Lisa Magro challenges us to answer life's greatest questions: Who is Jesus Christ?; Why you need a personal relationship with Him?; and How to have a walk with God? With great love for our Lord, she brings great biblical insight using God's Word in a relevant way. It is a message that each person desperately needs to hear.

Eric Stitts,
Senior Pastor
Bayside Baptist Church

The reality of eternity can be easily found inside the pages of this book. As Lisa's parents, we are proud of her achievements through Christ and pray that the Holy Spirit will open many hearts through the truth of this book, "The Door."

Larry and Anita Underwood

# THE DOOR

Amy,
"Glorify Jesus"

Lisa Underwood Magro

Lisa Underwood Magro

CROSSBOOKS
PUBLISHING

*CrossBooks*™
*A Division of LifeWay*
*1663 Liberty Drive*
*Bloomington, IN 47403*
*www.crossbooks.com*
*Phone: 1-866-879-0502*

*First published by CrossBooks 11/14/2011*

*ISBN: 978-1-4627-1176-5 (sc)*
*ISBN: 978-1-4627-1177-2 (e)*

*Library of Congress Control Number: 2011960260*

*Printed in the United States of America*

# ACKNOWLEDGEMENTS

I would first and foremost like to acknowledge the *Lord Jesus Christ,* who has given me the knowledge and understanding to write it. Thank you, Lord Jesus, for what have done for me. *Father God, Lord Jesus Christ and Holy Spirit – I love you!*

I would like to thank my husband, *Rick,* who has been extremely supportive and very understanding in my accomplishment of writing this book. *Michael,* my oldest stepson, has helped me with computer technicalities and has run errands. *Nick,* my youngest stepson, has supported me as well. *I love you all bunches and bunches.*

I am grateful to my parents, *Larry and Anita Underwood,* who have guided me throughout my life to follow the Lord Jesus. My father, who has been a faithful servant of God and who has preached for over 40 years, has helped me learn and understand the Bible. My mother, who has been a woman of God, has helped me learn and understand the Bible as well. Thank you both for your godly advice, support, prayer, and encouragement during the completion of this book. *I love you both so very much.*

I also want to thank all of my *family and friends* who have prayed for me and encouraged me through the writing of this book. *You will never know what you all mean to me.*

My pastor, *Eric Stitts, his wife, Amy* and their family prayed for me, encouraged me and gave me support as well. I am thankful for their desire to see people come to the saving knowledge of Jesus Christ. Also, I would like to thank *Martha Payne,* who was one of the first people to read the manuscript.

Thank you for taking the time to read it as well as for your recommendations. Additionally, I want to thank all of my *Bayside friends* for their prayers and encouragements. *All of you are a blessing*!

Thank you *Mark, Mara, Lacy, Brian, Sam* and *others* at Crossbooks Publishing Company for your kindness. You made the process of publishing my book smooth sailing. I am looking forward to publishing Genesis. *Again, many thanks!*

Lastly, thank you *Julie J. Van Valkenburg* for all the hours you spent editing my book. I know I drove you crazy. *You are a Pro!*

# FOREWORD

When Lisa was contemplating starting a Doctoral Program, I told her she would have to write a book. Her response was "You have to be kidding me!" Well, she did and she gives the Lord Jesus the glory for it. After all, it is His story.

From the beginning to the end, you will encounter Jesus Christ. The book is about Jesus, who He is, His life on earth and His future role.

She has also included several stories from our life adventures to illustrate her points. As I read the manuscript, I noticed she had not changed the names "to protect the innocent" and that many of our life events were included – both serious and humorous ones. I have to admit that all the stories are true and I was given little editorial review to delete any "sharing" of our life stories.

As you read this book, you will find both the information about Jesus' life and the interwoven stories of Lisa's experiences to be both energizing and uplifting. I am sure that you will find this book to be a blessing and you will have a better understanding of how Jesus can influence your life. You will see that He is "The Door."

Your loving husband,
Rick

## Dedication

### IN MEMORY OF RUTH HALL

I dedicate this book to the memory of Ruth Hall, my grandmother. I love you so much. For those of you who did not have the privilege of meeting my grandmother, you never would have forgotten her. I will never forget her sweet smile and her hugs. She was a godly woman and loved Jesus Christ. I had the honor of spending a great deal of time with her. She was such an inspiration to me. She constantly prayed for me. She was so precious to me. She fought the good fight and finished the course that God had given her to complete. I know that she is with the Lord and having the time of her life.

I love you, Grandma.

# CONTENTS

# INTRODUCTION

Heaven is a place where everyone wants to go – and with good reason. It is a perfect place built by a perfect person – Jesus Christ. It is also a prepared place. In John 14:1-3, it says, "Let not your heart be troubled; you believe in God, believe also in me. In My Father's house are many mansions; if it were not so, I would have told you. *I go to prepare a place for you.* And if I go and prepare a place for you, I will come again and receive you to Myself; that where I am, there you may be also."

Many people believe that there are many "doors," if you will, to heaven. Some people believe that if you obey the Ten Commandments, if you go to church, if you live a good life, if you have never done a "really" bad thing, if you grow up in a Christian family, or you are baptized, you will go to heaven.

Although these views may sound good, they are not biblical. The Bible does not support any of these views as means of acceptance into heaven. *There is only one Door to heaven, Who is Jesus Christ.*

In this book, I will show biblical support of why Jesus is the Only Door to heaven. In John 10:9, we read, "I am the Door. If anyone enters by Me, he will be saved, and will go in and out and find pasture."

My prayer is that whoever reads this book will be set free by the truth of who Jesus Christ is and why He is the only Door into heaven. "And you shall know the truth, and the truth shall make you free" (John 8:32).

# CHAPTER 1

## *JESUS CHRIST: WHO IS HE?*

*Who is Jesus Christ? Where did He come from? Has He always been? Will He always be?* We all have many questions about Jesus. I would like to answer these questions based on the Word of God. There is so much about Jesus to learn, as I am sure there is so much about Jesus that we will never know on this earth. Jesus Christ is the greatest person who has ever lived. No one can compare with Him. Jesus is the focal point of the Bible as well as the main theme of prophecy.

Charles Spurgeon, a British Baptist preacher, said of Jesus, "You may study, look and meditate, but Jesus is a greater Savior than you think Him to be, even when your thoughts are at their highest."

## *"WHO IS JESUS CHRIST?"*

Let's examine who Jesus Christ is. He is the second person of the Trinity, which consists of God the Father, God the Son (Jesus) and God the Holy Spirit. He is the perfect God-Man, which means that He is fully God and fully man. To clarify, He is perfect God because He is the second Person of the Trinity – God the Son. He is a perfect man (see 2 Corinthians 5:21) and without sin (see 1 John 3:5). Jesus became a man in the flesh. We read this in John 1:14. "And *The Word* became flesh and dwelt among us, and we beheld His glory, the glory

1

as of the only begotten of the Father, full of grace and truth." *The Word* is Jesus.

Dr. Charles Swindoll conducted an informal survey which included several men and women who were mainly in their twenties and thirties, well educated, and intelligent. During this interview, several of them were asked the question, "Who is Jesus?" Here are a few of the answers he received:

- Man 1: "That's a trick question." (Laughs) "I don't know how to answer that."
- Woman: "I mean, I believe that he was a real person and that he died on the cross, but I don't believe that he was God's Son."
- Man 2: "He was, you know – He was just another person that found religion and all that, so it's, I mean, He's nothing like, He's, of course, a good person and all that, and he's a really big part of religion, so, you know, all people that find religion are, you know, important. So people have different views."
- Man 3: "He is, uh – " (turns to younger man) "Help me out here." (young man shrugs) "Jesus Christ is, uh, the Son of God?" (looks again to the young man).[1]

You might have the impression that this interview took place in another country. However it occurred at a shopping mall in Frisco, Texas. According to the survey, Christians have quite a bit of witnessing to do for Jesus in the United States. It is a huge mission field for believers in Christ to reach the unsaved.

A couple of years ago, the senior citizens from my church went on a cruise. Our pastor and his wife joined them. While they were on the cruise, four teenage boys who were from the state of Maine accepted Christ. They had never been to church and did not know who Jesus Christ is. I believe that there are so many people just like them who desperately need to know who He is.

Let's see what Jesus said about who men say He is. In Mark 8:27-29 we read, "Now Jesus and his disciples went out to the towns of Caesarea Philippi; and on the road He asked His disciples, saying to them, 'Who do men say that I am?' So they answered, 'John the Baptist; but some say, Elijah; and others, one of the prophets.' He said to them, 'But who do you say that I am?' Peter answered and said to Him, 'You are the Christ.'" Peter recognized Him as being the Christ without hesitation. He knew who He was! He knew that Jesus was the Messiah!

If someone asked you who Jesus Christ is, would you answer quickly because you *know who He is?* Or, would you have to think about it? Moreover, if you know who He is, *do you know Him – personally? And do you know His voice?* You can! You can know Him better than you know your spouse, your parents, or your children. Do you want to know how? Let me explain through Scripture.

*Do you know Him personally?* First of all, God created you to know Him personally. However, there is a problem – sin. We are *all* separated from God because of sin. Let me clarify one thing: God loves the sinner, but not the sin.

When Jesus died on the cross, He took our sins on Himself and paid our debt that we could *never* pay. "But God demonstrates His own love toward us, in that while we were still sinners, Christ died for us" (Romans 5:8). Let that verse sink into your mind. "God demonstrates His own love toward us . . ." God loves us so much. It goes on to say "while we were still sinners, Christ died for us." Christ died around two thousand years ago. He died for us before we were even born. He knew that we would need a savior. Is He not amazing? He took care of our deepest need before we were even born.

As a result of Jesus Christ dying for sinners (us), He bridged the gap for a sinner to become a saint. This means when a sinner, who is someone separated from God or a lost person, is saved, they become a saint – a child of God. They are justified; "they have been made right with God."

Therefore, when a person prays to Jesus, admits that he or she is a sinner (Romans 3:23), asks Jesus to forgive him or her of their sins, believes that He died on the cross and paid his or her sin debt, believes that He arose again, and confesses Him as Lord and Savior (Romans 10:9), he or she is born again and becomes a child of God.

If you are born again, you are a child of God. "But as many as received Him, to them He gave the right to become children of God, to those who believe in His name: who were born, not of blood, nor of the will of the flesh, nor of the will of man, but of God" (John 1:12-13).

Understand that you are not automatically a child of God. Let's read the story of Nicodemus, who was a member of the Jewish ruling council (see John 3:1). In John 3:3-7 we read, "Jesus answered and said to him, 'Most assuredly, I say to you, unless one is born again, he cannot see the kingdom of God.' Nicodemus said to Him, 'How can a man be born when he is old? Can he enter a second time into his mother's womb and be born?' Jesus answered, 'Most assuredly I say to you, unless one is born of water and the Spirit, he cannot enter the kingdom of God. That which is born of the flesh is flesh, and that which is born of the Spirit is spirit.' 'Do not marvel that I said to you,' 'You must be born again.'"

Let's revisit John 3:6. "That which is born of the flesh is flesh, and that which is born of the Spirit is spirit . . ." When a person is born from human parents, they are born into sin and cannot save themselves because they are sinners.

However, when a person is spiritually born (born of the Spirit), which is to say, when a person trusts Jesus Christ as their Lord and Savior, this person is "born again" through the spirit. A born-again person receives a new nature and is made fit for the kingdom of God, or heaven.

Let's read John 14:16-17: "And I will pray the Father, and He will give you another helper, that He may abide with you forever – the spirit of truth, whom the world cannot receive, because it neither sees Him nor knows Him; but you know Him, for He dwells with you and will be in you."

Therefore, a born-again person has the living God inside of him or her through the Holy Spirit. The Holy Spirit is the helper whom Jesus promised to the disciples after His ascension into heaven.

When a person is born again or saved, he or she is regenerated. The word "regeneration" means "the spiritual change that is brought about in a person's life by an act of God." In regeneration, a person's sinful nature is changed, and this person is able to respond to God in faith. The literal meaning of regeneration is to be born again. As we discussed earlier, there are two births. The first birth is "of the flesh," and the second birth is "of the Spirit." Being born of the Spirit is essential before a person can enter the kingdom of God (heaven).[2]

The need for regeneration grows out of humanity's sinfulness. It is brought about through God's initiative. God works in the human heart, and each person responds to God through faith. Thus, regeneration is an act of God through the Holy Spirit, resulting in resurrection from sin to a new life in Jesus Christ.[3] The scripture teaches, "Therefore, if anyone is in Christ, he is a new creation; old things have passed away; behold all things have become new" (2 Corinthians 5:17).

So, in order for this regeneration to take place, each person has to have a relationship with Jesus Christ. "Jesus said to him, 'I am the way, the truth, and the life. No one comes to the Father except through Me'" (John 14:6).

If you are going to go to heaven, which is the place that Jesus is creating, you have to accept Him and Him alone as Lord and Savior.

5

Let me reiterate. Jesus said in John 14:2-4, "In my Father's house are many mansions; if it were not so, I would have told you. *I go to prepare a place for you.* And if I go and prepare a place for you, I will come again and receive you to Myself; that where I am, there you may be also. And where I go you know, and the way you know." The way to the place where He is going is through Him.

Jesus has to take a person to heaven because He knows where it is. He is creating heaven! This is stated in John 14:3. "And if I go and prepare a place for you, *I will come again and receive you to Myself; that where I am, there you may be also.*" What a comfort!

Additionally, let's read Revelation 21:22-23. "But I saw no temple in it, for the Lord God Almighty and the Lamb are its temple. The city had no need of the sun or of the moon to shine in it, for the glory of God illuminated it. The Lamb is its light." The Lamb is Jesus Christ.

In order to answer the next two questions, you have to know Jesus Christ personally, which was the first question. Let's go to the second question, *"Do you know Jesus' voice?"* In John 10: 27-30, it says, "My sheep hear My voice, and I know them, and they follow Me. And I give them eternal life, and they shall never perish; neither shall anyone snatch them out of My hand. My Father, who has given them to Me, is greater than all; and no one is able to snatch them out of my Father's hand. I and My Father are one."

My pastor, Eric Stitts, was preaching a series of sermons on "God Is Speaking . . . Are You Listening?" In one of his sermons, he said that there are three requirements in order to hear from God. They are:

1. You must have a *relationship* with the Shepherd, Jesus Christ as your Lord and Savior. He included that the Shepherd – Jesus – knows His sheep, those who have trusted in Him. He knows

their names and what they need. Furthermore, the Shepherd speaks to His sheep.

2. The Shepherd is *calling* you. He has a plan and a purpose for your life. The Shepherd provides for His sheep and He protects His sheep.

3. You *follow* the Shepherd! You should be obedient to Him.

Let's look at four characteristics of Jesus Christ as the Shepherd.

1. Christ showed that He was the *true* Shepherd (John 10:1-6). He was the true Shepherd because He had come to the fold in the way God had revealed in the Old Testament that His Shepherd would come.

2. Christ is the *good* Shepherd (John 10:7-11). According to Psalm 23, the role of the Shepherd was to make the sheep lie down in green pastures, to lead them beside quiet waters, to restore their souls, and to guide them in paths of righteousness. All this the good Shepherd did. Christ as the good Shepherd was Himself the way to life; and those who entered through Him were saved. They entered into freedom and found that which satisfied their souls.

3. Christ is the *only* Shepherd (John 10:12-16). Christ showed that He was the only true Shepherd because He knew His sheep; that is, He devoted Himself to their care. That they were the object of His loving concern as demonstrated by the fact that He was willing to sacrifice His own life in order to protect and preserve His sheep.

4. Christ is the *obedient* Shepherd (John 10:17-18). Christ viewed the sheep over which He had been appointed a Shepherd

as His Father's sheep. He came to the office of Shepherd by His Father's appointment. All that He did for the sheep, He did because He was faithful and obedient to His Father.[4]

So, how are we like sheep? Sheep are mentioned in the Bible about 750 times and more frequently than any other animal. The Bible makes many comparisons between the ways of sheep and human beings. The church, in the New Testament, is often compared to a sheepfold. The word "church" is defined as "a local assembly of believers as well as the redeemed of all ages who follow Jesus Christ as Savior and Lord."[5]

Because sheep in clusters are easily led, a single shepherd could watch over a large flock. By nature, sheep are helpless creatures. They depend on shepherds to lead them to water and pasture and to fight off wild beasts. Sheep are social animals that wander off and fall into crevices or get caught in thorn bushes. Then, the shepherd must leave the flock and search for the stray.

Jesus used this familiar picture when He described a shepherd who left ninety-nine sheep in the fold to search for one that had wandered off (see Matthew 18:12-14). Therefore, Jesus describes Himself as the good Shepherd who takes care of His sheep (John 10-1-18).[6] Charles Spurgeon said, "Now, let us commune together awhile upon the marks of the sheep. When there are so many flocks of sheep, it is necessary to mark them. Our Savior marks us. It has been very properly observed, that there are two marks on Christ's sheep. One is on the ear; the other is on their foot. These two marks of Christ's sheep are not to be found on any other; but they are to be found on all His own – the mark on the ear: 'My sheep hear my voice' – the mark on the foot: 'I know them and they follow Me.'"

He continues to say, "Think of this mark on their ear. 'My sheep hear my voice.' They hear spiritually. A great many people in Christ's day heard His voice who did not hear it in the way and with the perception that is intended here. They would not hear; that is to say, they would not hearken or give heed, neither would they obey His call or come unto Him that they might have life. The spiritual ear listens to God. When His sheep hear His voice, they know it so well that they can tell it at once from the voice of strangers."

Sheep are known for following only their shepherd's voice. In ancient times, many shepherds would lock together their folds of sheep for the night. The next morning each shepherd's flock would respond only to their shepherd's voice and be led to fields of green luscious grass.

Likewise, we who are saved follow only our Shepherd, Jesus. We will not follow another voice. Let's read John 10:4-5. "And when he brings out his own sheep, he goes before them; and the sheep follow him, for they know his voice. Yet they will by no means follow a stranger, but will flee from him, for they do not know the voice of strangers."

Charles Spurgeon went on to say, "Christ has marked his sheep on their feet as well as their ears. They follow Him; they are gently led, not harshly driven. They follow Him as the Captain of their salvation; they trust in the power of His arm to clear the way for them. All their trust on Him is stayed; all their hope on Him they lean."

Eddy McBroom, the student pastor at my church, preached one Sunday morning and gave four points in regards to "God Is Speaking . . . Are You Listening?" They are:

1. Listen and do *when it seems impossible* (Matthew 14:15-20).

2. Listen and do *when the journey's end is not known* (Mark 1:16-18).

3. Listen and do *when it looks too hard* (Luke 18:22-23).

4. Listen and do *when it does not make sense* (John 9:6-7).

Let's read John 10:27 again. "My sheep hear My voice, and I know them, *and they follow Me.*" If you are truly saved or born again, you will follow Christ. You will have a desire to follow Him. You will want to obey Him. You will want to live for Him.

Since we have been talking about listening to Him, do we in fact listen to Him and hear Him? I am reminded of when the Lord spoke to Samuel as a boy. Let's read of this account in 1 Samuel 3:1-10. "Now the boy Samuel ministered to the Lord before Eli. And the word of the Lord was rare in those days; there was no widespread revelation. And it came to pass at that time, while Eli was lying down in his place, and when his eyes had begun to grow so dim that he could not see, and before the lamp of God went out of the tabernacle of the Lord where the ark of God was, and while Samuel was lying down, that the Lord called Samuel. And he answered, 'Here I am!'

"So he ran to Eli and said, 'Here I am, for you called me.' And he said, 'I did not call; lie down again.' And he went and lay down. Then the Lord called yet again, 'Samuel!' So Samuel arose and went to Eli, and said, 'Here I am, for you called me.' He answered, 'I did not call, my son; lie down again.'

"(Now Samuel did not yet know the Lord, nor was the word of the Lord yet revealed to him.) And the Lord called Samuel again the third time. So he arose and went to Eli, and said, 'Here I am, for you did call me.' Then Eli perceived that the Lord had called the boy. Therefore Eli said to Samuel, 'Go, lie down; and it shall be, if He calls you, that you must say, 'Speak, Lord, for your servant hears.'" So Samuel went and lay down in his place.

"Now the Lord came and stood and called as at other times, 'Samuel! Samuel!' And Samuel answered, 'Speak, for Your servant hears.'"

The Lord wants us, as believers in Him, to listen and hear Him. He has plans that He wants to accomplish in and through us. In order for Him to accomplish this in us, we need to pray, read His Word and listen to what He is telling us to do.

Dr. Charles Stanley said, "If you will learn to listen to the Lord – and obey His voice – you will find an inexhaustible source of confidence, courage, strength and joy."

Let's return to John 10: 27-30. "My sheep hear My voice, and I know them, and they follow Me. *And I give them eternal life, and they shall never perish; neither shall anyone snatch them out of My hand. My Father, who has given them to Me, is greater than all; and no one is able to snatch them out of my Father's hand. I and My Father are one.*"

Think about it. " . . . And I give them eternal life, and they shall never perish; neither shall anyone snatch them out of My hand. My Father, who has given them to Me, is greater than all; no one is able to snatch them out of my Father's hand." Who is greater than God? No one. What comfort! I am safe and secure in Christ. Are you?

Now, let's talk about how we can know Jesus better. I am sure that there is a loved one in your life who you know quite well. In my case, that's Rick, my husband. Obviously, I am absolutely sure of what he looks like. I know his personality. Most of the time, he is happy and upbeat (except when I mention going to the mall). I know the places that he likes to vacation, one being Disney World. I know what he likes to eat, the "cowboy rib eye" at Ruth's Chris Steakhouse. I know what thrills him – using coupons. I have spent many years married to him and feel that I know him fairly well. At times, I can even think the way he thinks, which scares me. (Just kidding!)

Do you think that we can know Jesus that well? Absolutely. His disciples knew who He was, what He ate, and His attributes. They knew Him. I am not saying that they knew Him completely, but I believe that they knew

Him fairly well. One way we can know Him is by reading His Word, which is the Bible. He is *The Word*. "In the beginning was *The Word*, and *The Word* was with God, and *The Word* was God" (John 1:1). When we read His Word, we read all about Him.

The Bible guides us in how we are to live our lives, how to deal with others, how to discipline our children, how to handle problems and so much more. The Bible is the one book that we should read more than any other. It is full of knowledge.

Let's continue with our look at who Jesus Christ is. There are several names given to Him, which are biblically supported:

❖ *Jesus Christ is the advocate.* "My little children, these things I write to you, so that you may not sin. And if anyone sins, we have an Advocate with the Father, Jesus Christ the righteous" (1 John 2:1).

❖ *Jesus Christ is the almighty.* "'I am the Alpha and the Omega, the Beginning and the End,' says the Lord, 'who is, and who was, and who is to come, the Almighty'" (Revelation 1:8).

❖ *Jesus Christ is the atoning sacrifice for our sins.* "And He Himself is the propitiation for our sins, and not for ours only but also for the whole world" (1 John 2:2).

❖ *Jesus Christ the author and finisher of our faith.* "Looking unto Jesus, the author and finisher of our faith, who for the joy set before Him endured the cross, despising the shame, and has sat down at the right hand of the throne of God" (Hebrews 12:2).

❖ *Jesus Christ is the only begotten Son of God.* "No one has seen God at any time. The only begotten Son, who is in the bosom of the Father, He has declared Him" (John 1:18).

❖ *Jesus Christ is the chief cornerstone.* "Having been built on the foundation of the apostles and prophets, Jesus Christ Himself being the chief cornerstone" (Ephesians 2:20).

❖ *Jesus Christ is the creator.* "All things were made through Him, and without Him nothing was made that was made" (John 1:3).

❖ *Jesus Christ is the Door.* "I am the Door. If anyone enters by Me, he will be saved, and will go in and out and find pasture" (John 10:9).

❖ *Jesus Christ is eternal.* "And when I saw Him, I fell at His feet as dead. But He laid His right hand on me, saying to me, 'Do not be afraid; I am the First and the Last'" (Revelation 1:17).

❖ *Jesus Christ is faithful and true.* "Now I saw heaven opened, and behold, a white horse. And He who sat on him was called Faithful and True, and in righteousness He judges and makes wars" (Revelation 19:11).

❖ *Jesus Christ is the faithful witness.* "And from Jesus Christ, the faithful witness, the firstborn from the dead, and the ruler of the kings of the earth. To Him who loved us and washed us from our sins in His own blood," (Revelation 1:5).

❖ *Jesus Christ is God.* "In the beginning was the Word, and the Word was with God, and the Word was God" (John 1:1).

❖ *Jesus Christ is the good shepherd.* "I am the good shepherd. The good shepherd gives His life for the sheep" (John 10:11).

❖ *Jesus Christ is the great high priest.* "Seeing then that we have a great High Priest who has passed through the heavens, Jesus the Son of God, let us hold fast our confession" (Hebrews 4:14).

❖ *Jesus Christ is the great physician.* "Who Himself bore our sins in His own body on the tree, that we, having died to sins, might live for righteousness – by whose stripes you were healed" (1 Peter 2:24).

❖ *Jesus Christ is the "I am."* "Jesus said to them, 'Most assuredly, I say to you, before Abraham was, I am" (John 8:58).

❖ *Jesus Christ is the King of the Jews.* "Saying, 'Where is He who has been born King of the Jews? For we have seen His star in the East and have come to worship Him" (Matthew 2:2).

❖ *Jesus Christ is King of Kings and Lord of Lords.* "And He has on His robe and on His thigh a name written: 'King of Kings and Lord of Lords'" (Revelation 19:16).

❖ *Jesus Christ is the Lamb of God.* "The next day John saw Jesus coming toward him, and said, 'Behold! The

Lamb of God, who takes away the sin of the world!'" (John 1:29).

❖ *Jesus Christ is the last Adam.* "And so it is written, 'The first man Adam became a living being. The last Adam became a life-giving spirit'" (1 Corinthians 15:45).

❖ *Jesus Christ is life.* "In Him was life, and the life was the light of men" (John 1:4).

❖ *Jesus Christ is the light of the world.* "Then Jesus spoke to them again, saying, 'I am the light of the world. He who follows Me shall not walk in darkness, but have the light of life'" (John 8:12).

❖ *Jesus Christ is the lion of the tribe of Judah.* "But one of the elders said to me, 'Do not weep. Behold, the Lion of the tribe of Judah, the Root of David, has prevailed to open the scroll and to loose its seven seals'" (Revelation 5:5).

❖ *Jesus Christ is the living one.* "I am He who lives, and was dead, and behold, I am alive forevermore. Amen. And I have the keys of Hades and of Death" (Revelation 1:18).

❖ *Jesus Christ is Lord.* "And that every tongue should confess that Jesus Christ is Lord, to the glory of God the Father" (Philippians 2:11).

❖ *Jesus Christ is Lord of All.* "The word which God sent to the children of Israel, preaching peace through Jesus Christ – He is Lord of all" (Acts 10:36).

❖ *Jesus Christ is Lord of the dead and the living.* "For to this end Christ died and rose and lived again, that He might be Lord of both the dead and the living" (Romans 14:9).

❖ *Jesus Christ is Lord of the Sabbath.* "Therefore the Son of Man is also Lord of the Sabbath" (Mark 2:28).

❖ *Jesus Christ is the mediator between God and man.* "For there is one God and one Mediator between God and men, the Man Christ Jesus" (1 Timothy 2:5).

❖ *Jesus Christ is the morning star.* "I, Jesus, have sent My angel to testify to you these things in the churches. I am the Root and the Offspring of David, the Bright and Morning Star" (Revelation 22:16).

❖ *Jesus Christ is omnipotent, which means "all-powerful."* "And Jesus came and spoke to them, saying, 'All authority has been given to Me in heaven and on earth'" (Matthew 28:18).

❖ *Jesus Christ is omnipresent, which means "present everywhere."* "And He put all things under His feet, and gave Him to be head over all things to the church, which is His body, the fullness of Him who fills all in all" (Ephesians 1:22-23).

❖ *Jesus Christ is one with God.* "I and My Father are one" (John 10:30).

❖ *Jesus Christ is our Passover.* "Therefore purge out the old leaven, that you may be a new lump, since you truly are unleavened. For indeed Christ, our Passover, was sacrificed for us" (1 Corinthians 5:7).

❖ *Jesus Christ is the power of God.* "But to those who are called, both Jews and Greeks, Christ the power of God and the wisdom of God" (1 Corinthians 1:24).

❖ *Jesus Christ is the resurrection and the life.* "Jesus said to her, 'I am the resurrection and the life. He who believes in Me, though he may die, he shall live'" (John 11:25).

❖ *Jesus Christ is righteous.* "For He made Him who knew no sin to be sin for us, that we might become the righteousness of God in Him" (2 Corinthians 5:21).

❖ *Jesus Christ is the rock.* "And all drank the same spiritual drink. For they drank of that spiritual Rock that followed them, and that Rock was Christ" (1 Corinthians 10:4).

❖ *Jesus Christ is the root and the offspring of David.* "I, Jesus, have sent my angel to testify to you these things in the churches. I am the Root and the Offspring of David, the Bright and Morning Star" (Revelation 22:16).

❖ *Jesus Christ is the second man.* "The first man was of the earth, made of dust; the second Man is the Lord from heaven" (1 Corinthians 15:47).

❖ *Jesus Christ is the son of Abraham.* "The book of the genealogy of Jesus Christ, the Son of David, the Son of Abraham" (Matthew 1:1).

❖ *Jesus Christ is the son of man.* "And Jesus said to him, 'Foxes have holes and birds of the air *have* nests, but the Son of Man has nowhere to lay *His* head'" (Matthew 8:20).

❖ *Jesus Christ is the true vine.* "I am the true vine, and my Father is the vinedresser" (John 15:1).

❖ *Jesus Christ is the truth.* "And the Word became flesh and dwelt among us, and we beheld His glory, the glory as of the only begotten of the Father, full of grace and truth" (John 1:14).

❖ *Jesus Christ is with us.* "Behold, the virgin shall be with child, and bear a Son, and they shall call His name Immanuel, which is translated, 'God with us'" (Matthew 1:23).

❖ *Jesus Christ is the way, the truth and the life.* "Jesus said to him, 'I am the way, the truth, and the life. No one comes to the Father except through Me'" (John 14:6).

❖ *Jesus Christ is wonderful, counselor, mighty God, everlasting Father and the Prince of Peace.* "For unto us a Child is born, unto us a Son is given; And the government will be upon His shoulder. And His name will be called Wonderful, Counselor, Mighty God, Everlasting Father, Prince of Peace" (Isaiah 9:6).

❖ *Jesus Christ is the Word of God.* "He was clothed with a robe dipped in blood, and His name is called, The Word of God" (Revelation 19:13).

These are only some of the titles that belong to Jesus. After reading these names, we can see that Jesus Christ is the one and only! There is no one like Him nor will there ever be!

Let's talk about Jesus wanting to be our *savior*. Our world needs a savior. Moreover, we need a perfect savior, because we are so imperfect. We are a sinful and hopeless people. For that reason, Jesus, who knew we needed a savior, gave His life so that we, those of us who are born again, could live forever with Him. However, in the event that Jesus had not died and rose again, all of us would go to hell and be eternally separated from God. The reason is because we are sinners and our sin separates us from God.

For you see, heaven is a perfect place made for perfect people. The word "perfect" is defined as "without mistake, excellent or complete." It also means to be without sin. You may ask, "How do we know that we are sinners?" The Bible tells us so. In Romans 3:23, we read, "For all have sinned and fall short of the glory of God." In 1 John 1:8, we read, "If we say that we have no sin, we deceive ourselves, and the truth is not in us."

Also, 1 Kings 8:46 says, "When they sin against You (for there is no one who does not sin) and You become angry with them and deliver them to the enemy, and they take them captive to the land of the enemy, far or near;" You see, God is perfect, without sin. You may say, "Well, I do not sin nor do I have a sin problem." The Bible says that we *all* have sinned. As earlier noted, 1 John 1:8 says, "If we say that we have no sin, we deceive ourselves, and the truth is not in us."

Let's talk about what sin is. Sin is defined in James 4:17. "Therefore, to him who knows to do good and does not do it, to him it is sin." In addition, in 1 John 3:4 it says, "Whoever commits sin also commits lawlessness, and sin is lawlessness." As I stated earlier, when we break God's law, we sin.

Have you ever told a lie? Have you ever taken something, whether it was a pencil or a paper clip, that was not yours? Have you ever gossiped about someone? Have you ever thought a bad thought? Have you ever wronged someone? If so, you have sinned. If you commit one sin, you are a sinner – besides the fact that we are born sinners. All of us are under the judgment of God, unless you have trusted Jesus Christ as your Lord and Savior. Even Mary, Jesus' Mother, realized that she needed a savior. "And Mary said: 'My soul magnifies the Lord, and my spirit has rejoiced in God my Savior'" (Luke 1:46-47). We all need a savior who is Christ the Lord.

As I wrote earlier, we are born sinners. Let's read Romans 5:12. "Therefore, just *as through one man sin entered the world*, and death through sin, and thus death spread to all men, because all sinned . . . ." The "one man" in the verse is Adam.

Adam is portrayed in this verse as the federal head or representative of all those who are in the old creation. Christ is presented as the federal head of all those who are in the new creation. A federal head acts for all those who are under him. For example, when the president of a country signs a bill into law, he is acting for all the citizens of that country.[7]

This is what happened in Adam's case. As a result of his sin, human death entered the world. Death became the common lot of all Adam's descendants because they had all sinned in him. [8]

Someone might object that it was Eve and not Adam who committed the first sin on earth. That is true, but since Adam was the first to be created, headship was given to him. So he is seen as acting for all his descendants.[9]

Since we are sinners, we have a problem. For you see, God is holy, righteous and perfect. He has no sin in Him. None! We are separated from Him because of our sin. Therefore, we have a huge problem. So, what do we do about our sin problem? We know that we cannot save ourselves, because we are sinners. We have sin in us. We have a sin debt that we cannot pay. We need someone who is perfect and sinless.

Let's see who this person is. Let's see what happened when Jesus Christ was on the cross. In Matthew 27:46, it says, "And about the ninth hour Jesus cried out in a loud voice, saying, 'Eli, Eli, lama sabachthani?' that is, *'My God, My God, why have You forsaken Me?'*"

In this period of darkness, Jesus became the sin-offering for the whole world. At this point, God, His Father, forsook Him. Jesus felt a separation from His Father that He had never known, *for in becoming sin for us*, the Father had to turn away from His Son. *The Lord Jesus had no sin of His own, but He took our sins upon Himself.* He took our punishment. Let's read this in 2 Corinthians 5:21. "For He made Him who knew no sin to be sin for us, that we might become the righteousness of God in Him."

God cannot overlook sin. He does not take it lightly. He sent His only begotten Son, Jesus, who was sinless and perfect, to die a cruel death to pay for our sins. So, you may be wondering, "How do I get my sins forgiven, in order that I will not be separated from God?" There is only one way. The only way to have your sins completely forgiven is through Jesus Christ. For you see, if there had been any other way to accomplish this, Jesus would never have had to die on the cross.

Let's read John 3:16. "For God so loved the world that He gave His only begotten Son, that whoever believes in Him should not perish but have everlasting life." Let's also read Matthew 26:28. "For this is *My blood* of the new covenant, which is shed for many for the *remission of sins.*" Notice this verse says, *My blood* that means *Jesus' blood.* He shed His blood for many for the remission of sins. The *remission of sins* means *that your sins are absolved, pardoned, forgiven through the blood of Jesus.* If you have been born again, your sin debt has been paid in full not just partially paid, but in full.

This gift of salvation through Jesus Christ is a *free* gift. What is a gift? It is a free and unconditional present. A gift is the only basis on which God offers salvation. It is not earned. *It is through faith in Jesus Christ alone.* Faith means that a person realizes that he or she is a guilty, lost sinner and receives the Lord Jesus as his or her only hope of salvation.

In Ephesians 2:8-9 we read, "For by grace you have been saved through faith, and that not of yourselves; it is the gift of God, not of works, lest anyone should boast." The way that we receive this gift of salvation and eternal life is *through* faith.

As I mentioned earlier, if a person could be saved by doing good works, Christ did not need to die. Let's revisit Ephesians 2:9. "Not of works, lest anyone should boast." If someone could be saved by their works, they would have reason to boast before God. However, in Romans 3:27, it says, "Where is boasting then? It is excluded. By what law? Of works? No, but by the law of faith." Salvation can only come through faith in Jesus.

I recently read a story about a widow whose only daughter was very sick and in need of fresh fruit. But it was winter. Grapes and oranges were expensive and the widow was poor. Walking the streets of the city, the woman found herself outside the royal palace. She looked through the gate and saw in the royal greenhouse great clusters of the most appetizing and tempting grapes. As she gazed at them wistfully, the princess came by and, taking in the situation at a glance, with her own hands cut for the widow a magnificent basketful of fruit. With trembling hands, the widow offered the royal lady payment of the few coppers she had in her purse, but she received instead this noble reply, "Madam, these grapes are *not* for sale. My father is a king and he's much too rich to sell, and besides, you are much too poor to buy. You can have these grapes free or not at all!" That's it! Our Father is a King. He does not sell salvation. He offers salvation free or not at all. [10]

For you see, all of us are sinners. Not just a few of us, but all of us. (See Romans 3:23.) This includes all of Jesus' disciples and Jesus' family members. All of us have sinned, except of course Jesus. Even though salvation is a gift, which is offered to everyone (see John 3:16), it came at a costly price. God did not send His one and only Son, Jesus Christ, to die in vain.

The only way to heaven is through one person, Jesus Christ, and Him alone. He is the *only Door* to heaven!

Let's see who else recognized Jesus as savior. When Jesus was crucified, there were criminals on each side of Him. Let's see what we find in Luke 23:39-43. "Then one of the criminals who were hanged blasphemed Him, saying, 'If You are the Christ, save Yourself and us.' But the other, answering, rebuked him, saying, 'Do you not even fear God, seeing you are under the same condemnation?' 'And we indeed justly, for we receive the due reward of our deeds; but this Man has done nothing wrong.' Then he said to Jesus, 'Lord, remember me when You come into Your kingdom.' And Jesus said to him, 'Assuredly, I say to you, today you will be with Me in Paradise.'"

Let's pause here for just a moment. From this text, this second criminal recognized who Jesus was. "Then he said to Jesus, 'Lord, remember me when You come into Your kingdom'" (Luke 23:42). "And Jesus said to him, 'Assuredly, I say to you, today you will be with Me in paradise.'" (Luke 23:43). This criminal did not have time to do good works, to be baptized, or to go to church. He said to Jesus, "Lord, remember me when You come into Your kingdom," Jesus said to him, "Assuredly, I say to you, today you will be with Me in paradise" Luke 23:42-43. When this criminal died, he was with Jesus.

It is only the grace of God in the cross of Christ that can instantly transform a reviling sinner into an attitude of saving faith and confession. This repentant criminal began to see (1) the justice of his own punishment (v. 41); (2) the sinless character of Christ (v. 41); (3) the Deity of Christ (v. 42); (4) a living Christ beyond the grave (v. 42); and (5) a kingdom beyond the cross, with Jesus as its coming King (v. 42). [11]

Do you realize that Jesus did not have to leave heaven and come to this earth as a Perfect Man, and die the cruelest death for us? Yet He did! Why? Because He loves us! He knew that there was no other way to save us but through Himself.

In Matthew 26:39 we read, "He went a little farther and fell on His face, and prayed, saying, 'O My Father, if it is possible, let this cup pass from Me; nevertheless, not as I will, but as You will.'"

He was not asking to be delivered from going to the cross. That was the very purpose of His coming into the world! The prayer was rhetorical, that is, it was not intended to elicit an answer but to teach us a lesson. Jesus was saying in effect, "My Father, if there is any other way by which ungodly sinners can be saved than by my going to the cross, reveal that way now! But in all of this, I want it known that I desire nothing contrary to your will."[12]

What was the answer? There was none. The heavens were silent. By this eloquent silence we know that there was no other way for God to justify guilty sinners than for Christ, the sinless savior, to die as our substitute.[13]

He chose to die for us. *Jesus is also called the "King of Kings and Lord of Lords."* (See Revelation 19:16.) Just imagine the "King of Kings and Lord of Lords" dying for sinners. That means He died for us! We are so imperfect. If you think that you are a pretty good person, compare yourself to Jesus. A perfect king who knew no sin! He has never told a lie. He never gossiped. He never stole anything. He never said an unjust word. He never sinned. He is the perfect Lamb of God, and He loves you and me!

Has there been that time in your life when you have asked Jesus to save you? If not, I would encourage you to pray, "Lord Jesus, I know that I am a sinner. I know that there is no way that I can save myself. I am asking you to forgive me of my sins. I believe that you died on the cross in my place and rose again. Please save me now, Lord Jesus. I thank you for writing my name in the Lamb's Book of Life. In Jesus' name, I pray Amen."

If you have never asked Jesus to save you, you will miss it all. You will miss the most precious relationship that you will ever have on this earth, and you will miss heaven. When you are born again, it is the most important, most wonderful and most fulfilling decision that you will ever make. Jesus loves us immensely. Embrace that He loves you!

When a person accepts and receives Jesus Christ as Savior, the Holy Spirit comes and lives in them forever. They are sealed by the Holy Spirit of God. This is confirmed in Ephesians 1:13-14. "In Him you also trusted, after you heard the word of truth, the gospel of your salvation; in whom also, having believed, you were sealed with the Holy Spirit of promise, who is the guarantee of our inheritance until the redemption of the purchased possession, to the praise of His glory."

The Holy Spirit is the third person of the Trinity, which includes God the Father, God the Son, and God the Holy Spirit. The Holy Spirit is our seal that we are God's property. In 1 Corinthians 6:19-20, we read, "Or do you not know that your body is the temple of the Holy Spirit *who* is in you, whom you have from God, and you are not your own? For you were bought at a price; therefore glorify God in your body and in your spirit, which are God's."

Moreover, we read in John 14:26, "But the Helper, the Holy Spirit, whom the Father will send in My name, He will teach you all things, and bring to your remembrance all things that I have said to you." The Holy Spirit did this first through the spoken ministry of the apostles then through the Bible, which is the written Word of God.

Let me take a moment and say that a sinner's prayer is the first prayer that God hears from an unsaved person. If you are unsaved, lost without Jesus Christ, and have been praying to God your prayers have not been heard. Let's read John 9:31. "Now we know that God does not hear sinners; but if anyone is a worshiper of God and does His will, He hears him." And Romans 5:10 says, "For if when we were enemies we were reconciled to God through the death of

His Son, much more, having been reconciled, we shall be saved by His life."

Let's also read Isaiah 59:1-2. "Behold the Lord's hand is not shortened, that it cannot save; nor His ear heavy, that it cannot hear. But your iniquities have separated you from your God; and your sins have hidden His face from you, so that He will not hear."

In order to have peace with God, a person has to go through Jesus for salvation. Let's read Acts 4:12. *"Nor is there salvation in any other, for there is no other name under heaven given among men by which we must be saved." Jesus – the only one – not anyone else.* There is no other name that a person can go through to be saved. Let's read Matthew 1:21. "And she will bring forth a Son, and you shall call His name *Jesus*, for He will save His people from their sins."

When I think about Jesus and how vast He is, I am amazed every time I read Isaiah 66:1. *"Thus says the Lord: 'Heaven is My throne, and earth is My footstool.* Where is the house that you will build Me? And where is the place of My rest?" Let's picture in our minds a throne and a footstool. Now, consider the fact that Almighty God has the earth as His footstool!

Can you comprehend how big God is? Have you ever been in an airplane and looked down to see the cars on the freeways? The cars look like the miniature toy cars that children play with. Have you ever been on the 20th floor of a building and looked down and seen the people? Are they not tiny? Imagine God looking down from where He is!

With that in mind, think about how many people there are in the world. As of November 2010, the population of the United States was 310,691,217 and the population of the world was 6,881,104,426 as estimated by the United States Census Bureau. Now that, my friend, is a lot of people, and God knows how many hairs each of these 6,881,104,426 have on their heads. We read in Matthew 10:30, "But the very hairs of your head are all numbered." God knows every hair on our heads. Not just a couple. Every hair is numbered! I believe He knows even when we lose some.

He amazes me! What a God! What amazes me as well is that when I talk to Him, His line is never busy. He can hear me at anytime and anywhere! Let that soak into your mind. What a God!

Let's talk about Jesus being the *Bread of Life*. Let's read John 6:35. "And Jesus said to them, 'I am the bread of life. He who comes to Me shall never hunger, and he who believes in Me shall never thirst.'" Why do we eat bread? It sustains us. It gives us energy. It is good, especially homemade. We have to eat to live.

Likewise, Jesus is the believer's Bread of Life. He fills our spiritual hunger. Whereas bread fills our physical appetite, the Lord Jesus fills our spiritual appetite. In Matthew 4:4, it says, "But He answered and said, 'It is written, Man shall not live by bread alone, but by every word that proceeds from the mouth of God.'"

When you have a spiritual need, where do you go? Do you go to Christ and let Him provide for you what you need? We need to seek Him to meet our spiritual needs. If you have a child, when he is hungry, he comes to you wanting food. If you are a child of God, you need to go to Him to feed you spiritually. One way is in His Word. "For the bread of God is He who comes down from heaven and gives life to the world" (John 6:33). This is Jesus, the Bread of Life.

Here are some reasons why it is important for believers in Christ to spiritually feed on the Word of God or the Bible:

1. *The Bible is God's Word to us.* In 2 Timothy 3:16-17, we read, "All Scripture is given by inspiration of God, and is profitable for doctrine, for reproof, for correction, for instruction in righteousness, that the man of God may be complete, thoroughly equipped for every good work."

In 2 Peter 1:20-21, we read, "Knowing this first, that no prophecy of Scripture is of any private interpretation, for prophecy never came by the will of man, but holy men of God spoke *as they were* moved by the Holy Spirit." God moved men to write. It was not of their own doing. The Bible is literally God-breathed. In Isaiah 40:8, it says, "The grass withers, the flowers fades, but the word of our God stands forever." In addition, in Psalm 119:89, it says, "Forever, O Lord, Your word is settled in heaven." God's Word is eternal because He is eternal.

2. *We should read the Bible to distinguish between false teachings.* We live in a world that is inundated with false teachers and teachings. Therefore, it is of vital importance that believers in Christ know what they believe and that they know the Word of God.

In 1 John 4:1-3, we read, "Beloved, do not believe every spirit, but test the spirits, whether they are of God; because many false prophets have gone out into the world. By this you know the Spirit of God: Every spirit that confesses that Jesus Christ has come in the flesh is of God, and every spirit that does not confess that Jesus Christ has come in the flesh is not of God. And this is the *spirit* of the Antichrist, which you have heard was coming, and is now already in the world."

3. *We should read the Bible to find out what God says about how to live the Christian life.* Would it not make sense that if we are saved, we would want to know how He thinks and what He says in His Word about how we are to live? Let's see what God's Word says on some issues. For example, when we have sinned 1 John 1:9 states, "If we confess our sins, He is faithful and just to forgive us *our* sins and to cleanse us from all unrighteousness." If we want to know what the Bible says about fear of death, it is found in Psalm 23. If we want to know what we are to do if someone wrongs us, it is found in Colossians 3:13. These are just a couple of the many answers to our questions from the Bible.

4. *We should read the Bible to find out what God is like.* For example, in John 3:16, we find out that God loves us. In 1 Corinthians 1:9, we find out that He is faithful. In John 4:24, we find out that God is Spirit. In Psalm 46:1, we find out that He is our refuge and strength, a very present help in trouble. We find out in Hebrews 12:29 that God is a consuming fire.

The Bible is a book of answers, not a book of questions. It guides us in matters where the mind cannot penetrate, and where human reason leaves us unsatisfied.[14]

Let's talk about Jesus as our *comfort*. He knows when we are upset, crying or distraught before we tell Him. When I think of how Jesus knows us so well, I am reminded of Luke 10: 38-42. Let's read this section. "Now it happened as they went that He entered a certain village; and a certain woman named Martha welcomed Him into her house. And she had a sister called Mary, who also sat at the Jesus' feet and heard His word. But Martha was distracted with much serving, and she approached Him and said, 'Lord, do You not care that my sister has left me to serve alone? Therefore tell her to help me!' And Jesus answered and said to her, 'Martha, Martha, you are worried and troubled about many things. But one thing is needed, and Mary has chosen that good part, which will not be taken away from her.'"

He *knew* that Martha was worried and troubled about many things. He then tells her that only one thing is needed. What is that one thing? Listening to Jesus. Jesus brings us as believers comfort through His Word and through listening to Him. In the Bible, Jesus is telling us to listen to what He has to say. For example, in Mark 7:14, we read, "When He had called all the multitude to Himself, He said to them, 'Hear Me, everyone, and understand this:'"

Sometimes we want to listen to everyone but Jesus. We fail to seek Him. He is the first person who we should talk to and listen to. If you are a believer in Christ, He is there for you. In Matthew 11:28, we read, "Come to Me, all you who labor and are heavy laden, and I will give you rest." He tells us what to do when we are weary and burdened. Go to Him and He will give us rest. How comforting that is!

In today's society, people are looking for comfort. When we turn on the television or radio we hear of bombings, crimes, rapes, killings, wars, earthquakes, volcanoes erupting, and school shootings – just to name a few.

On February 16, 2011, a *USA Today* article was titled, "N.Y. Stock Exchange being bought by Germans." This article said, "The parent company of the New York Stock Exchange said Tuesday that it has agreed to be acquired by the operator of the Frankfurt stock exchange in a deal that will create the world's largest financial markets company."

With everything moving at such a fast pace in this world, we want to be comforted! We want someone to tell us that it will be okay. The good news is that we have that someone, Jesus. He wants to comfort those who have trusted Him. He is not in heaven wringing His hands in a panic.

On the contrary, He has everything under control. He knows exactly what has taken place on this earth. He knows what currently is taking place on this earth. Furthermore, He knows what will take place on this earth in the future. He is omniscient (all-knowing), omnipresent (everywhere), and omnipotent (all-powerful). He is God! The great "I am."

Earlier, I mentioned turning on the television and seeing reports of bad news, which included earthquakes. Let's pause a moment and think about earthquakes. A number are mentioned in the Bible, such as:

(1) At Mount Sinai (Exodus 19:18)

(2) Korah and companions destroyed in fissure and sinking ground (Numbers 16:31-33)

(3) In the Philistine camp in the days of Saul (1 Samuel 14:15)

(4) After Elijah's flight (1 Kings 19:11)

(5) In the reign of Uzziah, king of Judah (Zechariah 14:5)

(6) At Christ's death (Matthew 27:51-54)

(7) At Christ's Resurrection (Matthew 28:2)

(8) At Philippi when Paul and Silas were freed from prison (Acts 16:26)

Additionally, in Revelation 11:13, it says, "In the same hour there was a great earthquake, and a tenth of the city fell. In the earthquake seven thousand people were killed, and the rest were afraid and gave glory to the God of heaven." Let me point out that the earthquakes in the book of Revelation have not occurred yet.

The book of Revelation uses earthquakes as a symbol of the apocalyptic terrors of the end times – the upheavals in the religious and political realms which will precede and accompany the second coming of Christ (see Revelation 6:12). The Bible uses earthquakes as symbols of God's power (2 Samuel 22:8), presence (Psalm 68:8), revelation (Exodus 19:8), and judgments (Ezekiel 38:19-23).[15]

For example, I just cited the earthquake symbolizing God's power in 2 Samuel 22:8. Let's read this. "Then the earth shook and trembled; the foundations of heaven quaked and were shaken, because He was angry."

Lately, it seems that earthquakes are occurring everywhere. I did a little research on them. In 1935, Charles Richter, in partnership with Beno Gutenberg, both of the California Institute of Technology, developed the Richter Magnitude Scale. Richter's motivation for creating the local magnitude scale was to separate the vastly larger number of smaller earthquakes from the few larger earthquakes observed in California at the time. This method is still being used today.

The Richter magnitudes are as follows:

Less than 2.0 – micro earthquakes, not felt, about 8,000 per day.

2.0 - 2.9 – Generally not felt, but recorded, about 1,000 per day.

3.0 - 3.9 – Often felt, but rarely causes damage, 49,000 per year. (EST.)

4.0 - 4.9 – Noticeable shaking of indoor items, 6,200 per year. (EST.)

5.0 - 5.9 – Major damage to poorly constructed buildings, 800 per year.

6.0 - 6.9 – Can be destructive in areas up to about 100 miles, 120 per year.

7.0 - 7.9 – Can cause serious damage over larger areas, 18 per year.

8.0 - 8.9 – Can cause serious damage in areas several hundred miles long, 1 per year.

9.0 - 9.9 – Devastating in areas several thousand miles across, 1 per 20 years.

10.0 + – Never recorded. Extremely rare (Unknown).

The largest recorded earthquake in the world was the Great Chilean earthquake of May 22, 1960, which had a magnitude of 9.5. There were approximately 1,655 people killed, 3,000 injured, 2 million left homeless and $550 million damage in southern Chile. The tsunami caused 61 deaths, and $75 million damage in Hawaii, 138 deaths and $50 million damage in Japan, 32 dead and missing in the Philippines, and $500,000 in damage to the west coast of the United States.[16]

The five worst earthquakes in the world, along with their magnitudes[17], are listed below:

1. Valdivia, Chile. May 22, 1960. The magnitude was 9.5.

2. Prince William Sound, Alaska. March 27, 1964. The magnitude was 9.2.

3. Indian Ocean, Indonesia. December 26, 2004. The magnitude was 9.1-9.3.

4. Kamchatka, Russia. November 4,1952. The magnitude was 9.0.

5. Pacific Ocean, Japan. March 11, 2011. The magnitude was 9.0.

The magnitudes on these earthquakes are quite high. Let's look at the one that will take place in the future. In Revelation 16:18, it says, "And there were noises and thunderings and lightnings; and there was a great earthquake, such a mighty and great earthquake as had not occurred since men were on the earth." Of course, we have no idea what the magnitude will be, but it says " . . . a great earthquake, such a mighty and great earthquake as had not occurred since men were on the earth." It will be a terrifying one. I cannot imagine what it will be like.

If you are a believer in Christ, you know that He comforts us in Mark 13:7-8. "But when you hear of wars and rumors of wars, do not be troubled; for such things must happen, but the end is not yet. For nation will rise against nation, and kingdom against kingdom. And there will be earthquakes in various places, and there will be famines and troubles. These are the beginnings of sorrows." If you notice in verse 7, He tells us to not be troubled. He is bringing us comfort because He knows what is to come.

Now, let's talk about Jesus as our *counselor*. We see that He is our counselor in Isaiah 9:6. The definition of "counsel" is "to guide or to give advice." A Christian counselor, with the guidance of the Holy Spirit, can help guide people in how they should apply biblical concepts. Furthermore, the counselor can hold the person whom they are counseling accountable. Today, we see counselors everywhere: marriage counselors, drug abuse counselors, alcohol abuse counselors, school counselors, rehabilitation counselors, and child counselors, just to name a few.

We sincerely need counselors. However, they need to be saved counselors. There are times when believers in Christ need to seek godly advice through godly counselors. I thank the Lord for them. If you do need to speak with a counselor, pray that God would guide you to the counselor that He would have you go to. Be absolutely certain that the counselor is a believer in Jesus Christ. It matters who we ask for advice!

In 2 Samuel 2:1 we read, "It happened after this that David inquired of the Lord, saying, 'Shall I go up to any of the cities of Judah?' And the Lord said to him, 'Go up.' David said, 'Where shall I go up?' And He said, 'To Hebron.'" From this verse, we see that David was inquiring of the Lord about what cities of Judah to go to, and the Lord answered him specifically.

Has this ever happened to you? It has to me. When I have prayed specifically, He has answered specifically. For example, I knew that the Lord wanted me involved in a ministry of some kind. Therefore, I prayed about what He would have me to do. He made it crystal clear.

My grandmother was in the hospital, for her last visit, as she went to be with Jesus. I had come home that evening from being with her, and I had a message on the answering machine from my neighbor across the street. My friend referred her to me. She asked me to lead her women's Bible study group that following Saturday in her home. As a result, I have the privilege of leading and teaching women's Bible studies at my church. It has been a confirmation to me and I have received encouraging feedback as well.

As believers, we need to seek the Lord's advice on everything. We need to seek His advice on what car to buy, what house to purchase, what ministry He wants us to lead and so forth. Do you seek His advice? I am guilty of not doing this as often as I should. We need to begin our day in seeking His guidance about what He would have us to do on that day.

When a day is gone, it is gone. The opportunities that we had for that day are gone. We will never get them back. Let's read Galatians 6:10. "Therefore, as we have opportunity, let us do good to all, especially to those who are of the household of faith." When we ask for his direction and guidance as a believer, we need to remember that our lives are not our own. We were bought with a price.

In 1 Corinthians 6:19-20 it states, "Or do you not know that your body is the temple of the Holy Spirit *who* is in you, whom you have from God, and you are not your own? For you were bought at a price; therefore glorify God in your body and in your spirit, which are God's." It is not what we want to do but what He wants us to do. We should be obedient to Him. Jesus obeyed His Father even to the point of death. We who are saved should obey Him as well.

When we have trusted Jesus Christ as our Lord and Savior, we have the Holy Spirit of God indwelling us. *It matters where we go.* Wherever we go, the Holy Spirit of God goes. If you are in question about whether or not somewhere is an appropriate place to go, ask Him! I assure you that He will let you know.

*It matters what we say.* If there is something you want to say to someone but you are unsure how to say it or if you should say it, ask Him! Additionally, *it matters what we do*. If you want to do something and are not sure if it is the right thing to do, ask Him! *It matters where we go, what we do and what we say.*

If you are saved, do people see Jesus in you? One of my friends was going through a difficult time, and I had gone to visit her and took her a box of chocolate. Later, she sent me an e-mail saying, "You were Jesus to me last week." Our lives should reflect Jesus Christ.

When we encounter people who are hurting, who are unsaved, who are bitter, we need to show them Jesus. We, as believers in Christ, are His mouth, His hands, and His feet. We need to be a vessel that He can use! He has a purpose for each and every believer in Him. Are you doing what He has called you to do? Are you sold out to Jesus Christ?

Let's look at some of the people in the Bible. For example, Moses. God called him to lead the Israelites. God called David to be a king over Judah. God called Mary to be the vessel to bring Jesus into the world. God called Esther to save the Jews. He has a purpose and plan for your life as well!

Let's talk about Jesus as our *creator*. He created us. We are fearfully and wonderfully made. Let's read Psalm 139:14. "I will praise You, for I am fearfully and wonderfully made; marvelous are Your works, and that my soul knows very well." He made us!

Let's read Genesis 1:26-27 and see whose image we are made in. "Then God said, 'Let Us make man in Our image, according to Our likeness; let them have dominion over the fish of the sea, over the birds of the air, and over the cattle, over all the earth and over every creeping thing that creeps on the earth.' So God created man in His *own* image; in the image of God He created him; male and female He created them." Can you imagine that? We are the creation of Almighty God.

Let's talk about the body that He created. Let's have a quick lesson in basic anatomy. A human body has 206 bones, more than 650 muscles and ten major organ systems. The major organ systems are the: skeletal, muscular, circulatory, nervous, respiratory, digestive, excretory, endocrine, reproductive and the lymphatic/immune system. In addition, the body has many organs, with the skin being the largest.

In a single day, it is estimated that your heart beats 103,689 times, your blood travels 168,000,000 miles, the digestive system processes about 7.8 pounds of waste and the lungs take in 438 cubic feet of air. With this in mind, think about how intricately we are made.

Think about all the human organs and how they each have different functions within the body. We serve an awesome God, who created a magnificent human body!

No person has ever been born or will ever be born just like you. God created you unique from everyone else. No one has your personality, your views, your character, or your passions. You are you! God created you to be who you are!

Let's read Ephesians 2:10. "For we are His workmanship, created in Christ Jesus for good works, which God prepared beforehand that we should walk in them." The definition of "workmanship" is "the product or result of labor or skill."[18] We also read in Isaiah 64:8, "But now, O Lord, You are our Father; we are the clay, and You our potter; and all we are the work of Your hand."

As believers in Christ, He has equipped us with spiritual gifts. These gifts are listed in Romans 12:6-8. "Having then gifts differing according to the grace that is given to us, let us use them: If prophecy, let us prophesy in proportion to our faith; or ministry, let us use it in our ministering; he who teaches, in teaching; he who exhorts, in exhortation; he who gives, with liberality; he who leads, with diligence; he who shows mercy, with cheerfulness."

Sometimes when I am at the mall, I sit down and watch people. The way they walk, the way the talk, the way they look, the way they act – each one different. Our God is so amazing!

He created all 6,881,104,426 of us. All 6,881,104,426 of us are unique. We are all different. I can't even comprehend that many people, can you?

When I think about how the Lord God created me, I am amazed. For you see, I am an extremely hyper person. I am one person who does not need Starbucks coffee. I didn't say that I didn't like it. I said I didn't need it. I love the low-fat, decaf, white chocolate mocha. It is delightful!

God made me with hazel (sometimes brown) eyes and brown (most of the time blonde) hair. He made me unique. I am one of a kind and so are you. He knows all of my weaknesses and strengths. He knows what upsets me and he knows how to calm me down. He loves me! I have been through some pretty deep waters, but I can honestly say He has been with me all the way.

Let's talk about Jesus as our *friend*. What is a friend? Webster's Dictionary defines "friend" as "a close companion." A friend loves you for who you are and wants the best for you. A friend will never desert you when the going gets tough, but will go through it with you.

Jesus is the perfect friend. He understands your struggles; whether they are with insecurities, fears, or worrying. There is no trial, temptation, heartache, struggle or conflict that Jesus cannot identify with. In Hebrews 4:15 we read, "For we do not have a High Priest who cannot sympathize with our weaknesses, but was in all *points* tempted as *we are, yet* without sin."

Is He your friend? We usually spend time with our friends. We tell each other what is taking place in our lives. We enjoy their friendship. Likewise, do you spend time with Jesus? Do you tell Him about your day, whether it is good or bad? Do you tell Him about what is upsetting you? Do you thank Him for a blessing that he gave you? Sometimes, I find a parking space close to a building where I need to be. I thank Him for the parking space. It was a blessing to me. Instead, do you feel obligated to spend time with Him? He knows the difference.

Let's read John 15:15. "No longer do I call you servants, for a servant does not know what his master is doing; but I have called you friends, for all things that I heard from My Father I have made known to you."

He is the only friend I have that has ever died for me. He is truly a friend such as I have never met. He paid my sin debt that I could not pay. He met my greatest need; I needed a savior and so do you. I was on my way to hell, lost in my sins. "But God demonstrates His own love toward us, in that while we were still sinners, Christ died for us" (Romans 5:8). Remember, salvation is a gift. It is something that we do not deserve. It is grace! God's riches at Christ's expense.

I don't know about you but I just love talking to Him, praising Him, singing to Him, crying to Him, pleading with Him at times, walking with Him, being comforted by Him, and asking Him to calm me down when I am upset. If you are a believer in Jesus, have you ever thought about when you see Him face to face? I cannot imagine – my Savior – face to face with me!

On the other hand, have you ever felt like a person was your friend only to be betrayed by their friendship? Well, I have. When a person is supposed to be a friend and he or she betrays your friendship, it is very hurtful and your trust with them is broken. However, I know with Jesus, I don't have to worry about Him betraying me. Ever!

I can talk to Him at any hour of the day or night, because I know that He does not have an answering machine. I have a straight line to Him that is never busy! I can depend on Him to see me through anything that I encounter. I know that He will never leave me or forsake me.

If you are saved, you will never be separated from Him. He is your friend for life. Let's read Romans 8:38-39. "For I am persuaded that neither death nor life, nor angels nor principalities nor powers, nor things present nor things to come, nor height nor depth, nor any other created thing, shall be able to separate us from the love of God which is in Christ Jesus our Lord." There is nothing that will ever separate you from Him.

Even in death, a believer in Jesus is not separated from Him. Let's read this in 2 Corinthians 5:8. "We are confident, yes, well pleased rather to be absent from the body and to be present with the Lord." When I accepted Jesus Christ as my Lord and Savior, I received eternal life at that moment. Jesus will always be with me, even in death.

If you want someone who will never let you down, never leave you, never lead you down the wrong path, will always love you, and never betray your trust that person, my friend, is Jesus. In John 15:13 we read, "Greater love has no one than this, than to lay down one's life for his friends." What a friend we have in Jesus!

Let's talk about Jesus as our *great high priest.* If you have trusted Jesus as your Lord and Savior, He is your great high priest. A high priest in the Old Testament was distinguished from his fellow priests by the clothes he wore, the duties he performed and the particular requirements placed upon him as the spiritual head of God's people.[19]

His character and conduct was that he had to be without physical defect as well as holy in conduct. This is seen in Leviticus 21. The office of the high priest was hereditary. He could not show grief for the dead – even if it was his father or his mother – by removing his headdress or letting his hair go unkempt. He must not tear his clothes in grief or go near a dead body. Leaving his duties unperformed because of a death would "profane the sanctuary" (Leviticus 21:12). He could only marry a "virgin of his own people" (Leviticus 21:14). She could not be a widow, a divorced woman, or an impure woman. He must not, by a bad marriage, spoil his own holiness or endanger the holiness of his son who would succeed him.[20]

A high priest was consecrated (installed in office) by an elaborate seven-day service at the tabernacle or temple (see Exodus 29 and Leviticus 8). He was cleansed by bathing, and then dressed in the garments and symbols he must wear in his ministry and anointed with special oil.[21]

Sacrifices of sin offering, burnt offering, and consecration offering were made for him and he was anointed again with oil and with the blood of the sacrifice. Thus, sanctified to serve as a priest and consecrated to offer sacrifice (Exodus 28:41; 29:9), Aaron became "the saint (holy one) of the Lord" (Psalm 106:16).

The high priest's special garments represented his function as mediator between God and man. The high priests wore a white linen coat or tunic, dark blue woven robe, an ephod, which on each shoulder had onyx stones enclosed in pouches of gold with names of the twelve tribes engraved on them.

The ephod was made of fine linen interwoven with some threads of pure gold and other threads that were blue, purple, and scarlet in color.[22] Since Christ is our great high priest (Hebrews 8:1-6), the symbols in the ephod may be applied to Him. White linen speaks of His absolute righteousness. Scarlet (the color of blood) symbolizes His atoning work on the cross; purple, His royalty; gold, His divinity. Blue, the color of the sky, signifies Christ's origin with God the Father in Heaven. [23]

"And you shall put the two stones on the shoulders of the ephod as memorial stones for the sons of Israel. So Aaron shall bear their names before the Lord on his two shoulders as a memorial" (Exodus 28:12).

The "breastplate of judgment" was attached to the front of the ephod (Exodus 28:15-30). On the front of it were twelve precious stones engraved with the names of the twelve tribes. In its pocket, directly over his heart, were the Urim and Thummim (Exodus 30). These were gems or stones that were carried by the high priest and used to determine God's will in certain matters.

The robe of the ephod was a blue garment worn underneath the ephod. It extended below the knees (see Exodus 28:31-35). "You shall make the robe of the ephod all of blue. There shall be an opening for his head in the middle of it; it shall have a woven binding all around its opening, like the opening in a coat of mail, so that it does not tear. And upon its hem you shall make pomegranates of blue, purple, and scarlet, all around its hem, and bells of gold between them all around: a golden bell and a pomegranate, a golden bell and a pomegranate, upon the hem of the robe all around. And it shall be upon Aaron when he ministers, and its sound will be heard when he goes into the holy place before the Lord and when he comes out, that he may not die" (Exodus 28:33-35).

On his forehead, the high priest wore the holy crown of gold engraved with the words, "Holiness to the Lord" (Exodus 28:36-37). "So it shall be on Aaron's forehead, that Aaron may bear the iniquity of the holy things which the children of Israel hallow in all their holy gifts; and it shall always be on his forehead, that they may be accepted before the Lord" (Exodus 28:38).

There were certain functions given only to the high priest. God chose him to be the ultimate mediator between Him and the Israelites. He alone wore the Urim and the Thummim. Israel came to him to learn the will of God (see Deuteronomy 33:8). Only he could officiate and conduct certain ceremonies.

However, the most important responsibility of the high priest was to conduct the service on the Day of Atonement, the tenth day of the seventh month each year. It was the recognition of man's inability to make any atonement for his sins. It was a solemn and holy day. The Day of Atonement is explained in depth in Leviticus 16.

Let's read Leviticus 16 beginning with verse 3. "Thus Aaron shall come into the *Holy Place*: with the blood of a young bull as a sin offering, and of a ram as a burnt offering." The high priest, who officiated on this day, first sanctified himself by taking a ceremonial bath and putting on white garments (see verse 4). In verse 5, we read, "And he shall take from the congregation of the children of Israel two kids of the goats as a sin offering, and one ram as a burnt offering."

Verse 6 says "Aaron shall offer the bull as a sin offering, which is for himself, and make atonement for himself and for his house." Notice that the high priest had to make atonement for his sins as well. In today's society ministers, the Pope, the President of the United States – all of us have to have our sins forgiven through Jesus Christ and Him alone.

Let's read Leviticus 16:7-10. "He shall take the two goats and present them before the Lord at the door of the tabernacle of meeting. Then Aaron shall cast lots for the two goats: one lot for the Lord and the other lot for the scapegoat. And Aaron shall bring the goat on which the Lord's lot fell, and offer it as a sin offering. But the goat on which the lot fell to be the scapegoat shall be presented alive before the Lord, to make atonement upon it, and to let it go as the scapegoat in the wilderness."

Let's also read Leviticus 16:11-16. "And Aaron shall bring the bull of the sin offering, which is for himself, and make atonement for himself and for his house, and shall kill the bull as the sin offering which is for himself. Then he shall take a censer full of burning coals of fire from the altar before the Lord, with his hands full of sweet incense beaten fine, and bring it inside the veil.

"And he shall put the incense on the fire before the Lord, that the cloud of incense may cover the mercy seat that is on the Testimony, lest he die. He shall take some of the blood of the bull and sprinkle it with his finger on the mercy seat on the east side; and before the mercy seat he shall sprinkle some of the blood with his finger seven times. Then he shall kill the goat of the sin offering, which *is* for the people, bring its blood inside the veil, do with that blood as he did with the blood of the bull, and sprinkle it on the mercy seat and before the mercy seat. So he shall make atonement for the *Holy Place*, because of the uncleanness of the children of Israel, and because of their transgressions, for all their sins; and so he shall do for the tabernacle of meeting which remains among them in the midst of their uncleanness."

Let's read verses 20-21. "And when he has made an end of atoning for the *Holy Place*, the tabernacle of meeting, and the altar, he shall bring the live goat. Aaron shall lay both his hands on the head of the live goat, confess over it all the iniquities of the children of Israel, and all their transgressions, concerning all their sins, putting them on the head of the goat, and shall send it away into the wilderness by the hand of a suitable man."

Now, let's see what happens to this goat. The man took the goat and led it outside the camp, past the furthest tent, on out into the wilderness. On and on, farther and farther, until the camp of Israel was left far behind. It was a blur on the distant skyline. It disappeared altogether below the horizon. On and on they went, the sin-bearer and the fit (or suitable) man. At last, "in a land not inhabited," the man let the creature go and retraced his steps. The goat watched him disappear, bleated, and looked around. There was not a blade of grass, not a drop of water. The merciless sun beat down upon the head of the sin-bearer. Its strength was dried up like a potsherd. There was no eye to pity, no arm to save. It died alone, bearing the sin of all.[24]

The two goats that are mentioned in verse 7 symbolize two different aspects of atonement: "that which meets the character and holiness of God, and that which meets the need of the sinner as to the removal of his sins."[25]

Therefore, on the Day of Atonement, the high priest alone entered the *Holy Place* inside the veil before God. God dwelt on the Mercy Seat in the Temple, but no person could approach it except through the mediation of the high priest, who offered the blood of the sacrifice.

Let's pause here for just a moment. Let's observe the layout of the earthly tabernacle. The tabernacle had three main sections: the courtyard, the Holy Place and the Most Holy Place. The tabernacle tent had two rooms: the Holy Place was the larger room, which was the place that contained "The Golden Lampstand," "The Altar of Incense," and "The Table of the Bread of the Presence."

The *Most Holy Place,* which was also known as the Holy of Holies, was where God's presence dwelt. This place contained the ark of the Covenant. A veil divided the *Holy Place* from the *Most Holy Place.* The priests would minister on a daily basis in the *Holy Place.* However, only the High Priest could enter the *Most Holy Place* once a year on the Day of Atonement.

On the day of the Lord Jesus Christ's crucifixion, the veil in the temple was torn in two from top to bottom. Let's read this in Matthew 27:50-51. "And Jesus cried out again with a loud voice, and yielded up His spirit. Then, behold, the veil of the temple was torn in two from top to bottom; and the earth quaked, and the rocks were split." When He died, the veil was torn. It was as if a great hand reached down and tore it in two from top to bottom. Up until then, this veil had kept everyone, except the high priest, from entering the *Most Holy Place* or the *Holy of Holies* where God dwelt.

In the book of Hebrews, we learn that the veil represented the body of Christ. Let's read Hebrews 10:20. "By a new and living way which He consecrated for us, through the veil, that is, His flesh . . ." When Christ died, believers in Him were able to enter through Him to the *Holy of Holies* in the presence of God.

Let's read about this in Hebrews 10:19-22. "Therefore, brethren, having boldness to enter the Holiest by the blood of Jesus, by a new and living way which He consecrated for us, through the veil, that is, His flesh, and having a High Priest over the house of God, let us draw near with a true heart in full assurance of faith, having our hearts sprinkled from an evil conscience and our bodies washed with pure water."

Through Moses, God gave the law, which was a system in which blood atonement was made through blood offerings pointing man to the one time offering of Christ death on the cross. The Old Testament believers were looking to the cross and we are looking back at the cross.

The comparisons of Jesus as the High Priest and the High Priest on the Day of Atonement are listed below:

1. *Jesus is the Lamb of God and the perfect sacrifice* (see John 1-29, 36). In comparison to the high priest, who took a young bull and a ram to the altar, to offer for himself and two goats for the nation (see Leviticus 16).

2. *Jesus is the pure and sanctifying living water* (see John 4:10-15). In comparison to the high priest, who washed himself in the living (running) water of the bronze laver before putting on his garments and offering the sacrifices needed to enter the most Holy Place (see Leviticus 16:4).

3. *Jesus is our life-sustaining bread of heaven and covenant meal* (see John 6:35, 48-51). In comparison to the table of the bread of presence or the showbread in the Holy Place (see Exodus 25:30).

4. *Jesus is the light of the world.* He lights our path in darkness (see John 8:12). In comparison to the golden lampstand that provided light for the priests (see Exodus 25:37).

5. *Jesus, our great high priest, has and is praying for us before God the Father* (see John 17: 1-26). In comparison to the high priest approaching the altar of incense in front of the veil. He

took coals and incense and burned them in the *Most Holy Place* before God in prayer (see Leviticus 16: 12-13).

6. *Jesus is our atonement* (see Romans 3:25). He offered His own blood on our behalf (see 1 John 2:2). In comparison to the high priest, when he sprinkled the blood of the bull and the blood of one of the goats upon the Mercy Seat (see Leviticus 16:14-16).

7. *Jesus ministers in the Holy Place on our behalf* (see Revelation 1:12-20). In comparison to the high priest who sprinkled blood in the *Holy Place* and upon its furniture (see Leviticus 16:16-17).

8. *The heavenly altar declares God's ways true and just* (see Revelation 16:7). In comparison to the priest who sprinkled the bronze altar with blood (see Leviticus 16:18-19).[26]

Let's examine the reasons that Jesus is our great high priest:

1. He became man, which was of the seed of Abraham (Hebrews 2:11-18).

2. He is sympathetic with our weaknesses (Hebrews 4:15).

3. He did not assume the office of high priest for glory (Hebrews 5:5), but was called by God to the office.

4. He had no need, as the sons of Aaron, to offer sacrifices for His own sins, and then for the sins of the people, for He had no sin (Hebrews 7:27-28).

5. He offered His own blood (Hebrews 9:12) once for all (Hebrews 9:26; 10:10, 12) whereas they offered animal blood that could never take away sin (Hebrews 10:1-4).

6. His priesthood is eternal because He lives forever (Hebrews 7:25). They were many priests, because they died (Hebrews 7:23).

7. He performs His ministry in heaven (Hebrews 4:14; 9:11), seated at the right hand of God (Hebrews 10:12) whereas their priesthood was performed in an earthly model of the real sanctuary (Hebrews 8:5).

He is our great high priest. "Therefore, in all things He had to be made like *His* brethren, that He might be a merciful and faithful High Priest in things *pertaining* to God, to make propitiation for the sins of the people" (Hebrews 2:17).

If you have trusted Jesus Christ as your Lord and Savior, you have a high priest who knows what you go through, knows your weaknesses and your temptations. He was tempted as we are, yet He did not sin. He understands us and therefore is able to comfort us and loves us with such an awesome love. Hebrews 4:15 states, "For we do not have a High Priest who cannot sympathize with our weaknesses, but was in all *points* tempted as *we are*, yet without sin."

He wants to be, desires to be, and is capable of being everything to you! We just need Jesus – period! As Anne Graham Lotz says, "Just Give Me Jesus." He is all anyone has ever needed, presently needs, or will ever need!

Let's talk about Jesus as our *great physician*. In the Bible, we read about Jesus healing people. He healed people then and He heals people today. He is our great physician. I can certainly attest to His healing power. I have been anointed by oil three times in my life and healed. The Lord says in James 5:14-15, "Is anyone among you sick? Let him call for the elders of the church, and let them pray over him, anointing him with oil in the name of the Lord. And the prayer of faith will save the sick, and the

Lord will raise him up. And if he has committed sins, he will be forgiven."

The last time that I was anointed with oil was when I had melanoma in 2006. I am so thankful that the Lord allowed it to be found early and that it was not in a stage of the disease.

We need to realize that He is the great physician! If you are someone who needs to be healed, have you obeyed His Word and been anointed with oil? He tells us to do this in James 5:14-15. However, as believers in Christ, we need to understand that He may choose to heal us here on the earth or He may take us home to heaven. If someone is healed it is because Jesus healed them.

Furthermore, we read in Psalm 103:3, "Who forgives all your iniquities, who heals all your diseases."

We also see in Mark 5:25-34 of a woman with a blood sickness. "Now a certain woman had a flow of blood for twelve years, and had suffered many things from many physicians. She had spent all that she had and was no better, but rather grew worse. When she heard about Jesus, she came behind *Him* in the crowd and touched his garment. For she said, 'If only I may touch His clothes, I shall be made well.'

Immediately the fountain of her blood was dried up, and she felt in *her* body that she was healed from her affliction.

And Jesus, immediately knowing in Himself that power had gone out of Him, turned around in the crowd and said, 'Who touched My clothes?' But His disciples said to Him, 'You see the multitude thronging You and You say, 'Who touched me?' And He looked around to see her who had done this thing. But the woman, fearing and trembling, knowing what had happened to her, came and fell down before Him and told Him the whole truth. And He said to her, 'Daughter, your faith has made you well. Go in peace and be healed from your affliction.'"

Let's pause here for just a moment. Look at the faith of this woman in this story. She knew that if she touched His garment, she would be made well. She knew and recognized who Jesus was. We need to realize and understand that Jesus knows the sickness we will go through in our lives. Is that not comforting? Our God knows us and He knows us well! Why does He know us well? He created us!

Furthermore, we read about Hezekiah in 2 Kings 20:1-6, "In those days Hezekiah was sick and near death. And Isaiah the prophet, the son of Amoz, went to him and said to him, 'Thus says the Lord: Set your house in order, for you shall die, and not live.' Then he turned his face toward the wall, and prayed to the Lord, saying, 'Remember now, O Lord, I pray, how I have walked before You in truth and with a loyal heart, and have done what was good in Your sight.' And Hezekiah wept bitterly.

"And it happened, before Isaiah had gone out into the middle court, that the word of the Lord came to him, saying, 'Return and tell Hezekiah the leader of My people,' 'Thus says the Lord, the God of David your father: I have heard your prayer, I have seen your tears; surely I will heal you. On the third day you shall go up to the house of the Lord. And I will add to your days fifteen years. I will deliver you and this city from the hand of the king of Assyria; and I will defend this city for My own sake, and for the sake of My servant David.'"

We see from verse 5 that the Lord heard his prayer and He saw his tears. The Lord heard his prayer. How encouraging to us! When I see in verse 5, ". . . I have seen your tears . . ." I think of Psalm 56:8: "You number my wanderings; put my tears into Your bottle; Are they not in Your book?" He puts our tears in a bottle. He knows when we cry, how long we cry, and why we cry. He knows our sorrows! However, in heaven there will be no more tears and no more sorrows. "And God will wipe away every tear from their eyes; there shall be no more death, nor sorrow, nor crying. There shall be no more pain, for the former things have passed away" (Revelation 21:4). If you are born again, you have so much to look forward to in heaven. Praise His Name!

Let's talk about Jesus as our *Lord*. He knows what is best for us in every circumstance that we will ever encounter. He knows what we have done, what we are currently doing and what we will do.

Jesus Christ is Lord, whether a person wants Him to be or not. In Philippians 2:10-11, we read, "That at the name of Jesus every knee should bow, of those in heaven, and of those on earth, and of those under the earth, and that every tongue should confess that Jesus Christ is Lord, to the glory of God the Father."

On this earth, there are people who do not want to bow their knees before the Lord Jesus Christ, but one day they will and confess that Jesus Christ is Lord to the glory of God the Father. It will not be optional. What a wonderful time for believers in Christ to bow our knees and confess that He is Lord! It is such an honor and a privilege to bow our knees and confess that Jesus Christ is Lord now and what a "Lord" He is!

As Dr. Adrian Rogers said, "If there were only three words that we would be allowed to speak, those three words should be, 'Jesus is Lord!' There is no middle ground for the Christian: Jesus must be Lord of all or He can't be Lord at all." Jesus is called "Lord" no less than 747 times in the New Testament.

Have you submitted to His Lordship in your life? The definition of "submit" is "to yield."[27] Have you yielded your life to the Lordship of Jesus Christ? Is He Lord over every part of your life? On the other hand, are you holding on to parts of your life that you want to be in control of? As believers in Christ, we are servants to Him. He is our Lord.

If you are a believer in Jesus, He owns 100 percent of you. He does not own 10 percent or 50 percent but 100 percent! We are not our own. We were bought at a price. (See 1 Corinthians 6:19-20.)

When you submit to the Lordship of Christ, you are in essence saying that you surrender to His authority. You want to live a life of obedience to Him. Please understand that in your own self, this is impossible to accomplish. If a believer in Jesus wants to be obedient, they must rely on the power of the indwelling of the Holy Spirit. In John 14:16-17 we read, "And I will pray the Father, and He will give you another Helper, that He may abide with you forever – the Spirit of truth, whom the world cannot receive, because it neither sees Him nor knows Him; but you know Him, for He dwells with you and will be in you."

Have you asked the Lord Jesus what His purpose is for your life? I feel like His purpose for my life is to help women grow in His Word. I want to fulfill this purpose that I believe He has called me to do. You know, when I get to heaven, I want Him to say, "Well done good and faithful servant." We read this in Matthew 25:21. "His lord said to him, 'Well done, good and faithful servant; you were faithful over a few things, I will make you ruler over many things. Enter into the joy of your lord.'"

In the past, I have competed in running 5K (3.1 miles) road races, 10K (6.2 miles) road races, a half marathon (13.1 miles), and a marathon (26.2 miles). I always wanted to be the first-place winner. I usually got second or third place, which was okay. However, I desired first place. Likewise, I want to be the best at what the Lord Jesus has called me to do. My goal is 2 Timothy 4:7. "I have fought the good fight, I have finished the race, I have kept the faith." I want to hear, as I stated earlier, "Well done good and faithful servant" from Jesus.

When we think of trying to live a life of obedience on our own – it will not work. It will not happen simply because we want to "do it." We, as believers in Christ, are still in the flesh. We are subject to sinful conduct because we have a sinful nature. "For I know that in me (that is, in my flesh) nothing good dwells; for to will is present with me, but how to perform what is good I do not find. For the good that I will to do, I do not do; but the evil I will not to do, that I practice" (Romans 7:18-19).

Have you experienced this as a Christian? Have you had thoughts that you did not want to think? And you wonder "Why am I thinking this?" I have. Have you ever done something that was wrong? Then you think, "Why did I do that?" I believe we all have. Let me reiterate that we are subject to sinful conduct because we have a sinful nature.

However, as believers in Christ, we can live a life of obedience through the empowerment of the Holy Spirit, who dwells in us. Therefore, it is not in our power, but in His power. He enables us to live the Christian life. When a believer in Christ is submitting his life to Him, the Holy Spirit gets more of the believer. When a believer in Christ is filled with the Holy Spirit, he is yielding to the Spirit's control and not his own control.

For you see, if you are a believer in Christ, you are at your strongest when you are relying on Him and not yourself. "Therefore I take pleasure in infirmities, in reproaches, in needs, in persecutions, in distresses, for Christ's sake. For when I am weak, then I am strong" (2 Corinthians 12:10).

Let me introduce to you my mother, Anita Underwood. She is the epitome of Jesus. She illuminates Him in her life. In her actions, her words, her personality, her advice she truly displays Christ in her life. She loves Him. She is a godly woman. Likewise, as I have observed her life, I want to be the godly woman that Christ would have me to be.

On occasions, my mom has told me, in love, that I needed an "attitude adjustment." For the most part, I am an upbeat and joyful person. I love Jesus and strive to live my life in obedience to Him. I want to please Him above all.

However, there are times when I am ill-tempered and just flat out in a bad mood. You know kind of like "Eyeore, doom and gloom." Let me just say, I had rather be a Tigger. Have you ever had these doom and gloom days? You know the kind of days when you wake up, your spouse snored all night long or you had too much caffeine the day before and could not sleep. You just don't feel good. Then to top it off, your husband is singing "Zip-a-dee-doo-dah, zip-a-dee-ay, my, oh my, what a wonderful day!" Let's face it – that is the last thing that you want to hear is happy people! Much less your husband!

Have you ever heard the saying "Misery loves company?" Well, I have to admit that when I am not happy, I do not want anyone else to be happy. When I see that my moods and my emotions are not pleasing to the Lord, I ask for His help. (I will be honest, there are times I have forgotten too.) He comes to my rescue! He wants us to ask Him for help.

We see this in Luke 11:9-10. "So I say to you, ask, and it will be given to you; seek, and you will find; knock, and it will be opened to you. For everyone who asks receives, and he who seeks finds, and to him who knocks it will be opened." As a believer in Christ, ask Him to help you! He already knows everything about you anyway.

Let's talk about trouble or difficulty in our daily lives. Let's face it, we have days when the car won't start, the kids miss the bus, the house is a mess, the boss is yelling, you can't please your spouse, and so on. I have great news: Jesus wants to be your *present help in trouble.*

Let me tell you a story of Jesus being my present help in trouble. My husband, Rick, is the most wonderful husband in the world. His jobs in the past have required travel, which at times has been overwhelming for me. I have accompanied him on many trips. Now, let me tell you, I used to love to fly. I mean, if someone said "Let's go," my bags were packed.

The first year of our marriage, we flew quite a bit. If you fly Delta often, I am confident that you are aware of the MQM's, which are the Medallion Qualifying Miles that are used to determine SkyMiles Medallion status.

The levels are: Silver (25,000 MQM's or 30 segments), Gold (50,000 or 60 segments), Platinum (75,000 or 75,000 segments) and Diamond (125,000 or 140 segments). Could you just imagine flying so much that you qualified for Diamond status? Now, at the beginning of our marriage, I was Silver status and my husband was Platinum. I knew that the Silver status was the lowest status to have, but that was okay with me.

One of the flights that stands out in my mind was on September 7, 2001. We were flying out of Cincinnati, Ohio. Now, this particular evening all flights, due to inclement weather, were cancelled but ours. We had left from Cincinnati enroute to Salt Lake City, Utah. This flight was the most frightening of all the flights I have ever flown. The plane had about 250 passengers. I believe the pilot must have been ill because he kept going back and forth to the restroom. The flight attendants pretty much stayed in their seats, which is never a good sign!

My husband would look out the window and tell me of the storms. He was so excited! It was lightning and thundering, which you know just excited me to no end. The food, which was on the trays on the plane, was bouncing up and down. I wanted to crawl under the seat. Therefore, I prayed, prayed, and prayed. The Lord reminded me of Mark 4:37-41 when He calmed the storm. Jesus knew where I was! He knew that I was in a plane on my way to Salt Lake City in a terrible storm.

How many times do we forget that He knows where we are? He knows the storms that we are in. How do we face the storms of life? Is our faith strong in Christ or do we look at our circumstances?

Thankfully, the Lord landed the plane that night. Then, several days later, we were scheduled to fly out of Utah on the morning of September 11, 2001. On that morning, we got up, got packed and got on the airport shuttle bus, which had a television headed to the airport. That is when it happened! We saw the planes hit the Twin Towers in New York!

We got to the airport and went up to the ticket counter to check in. When we got there, we were notified that all flights had been grounded. Therefore, my husband went immediately to the rental car counter and tried to get us a car, which was a great idea. They told him that he had to have a reservation. Basically, no reservation – no car. I started praying. I pray quite a bit, by the way.

He called Unum, which was where he was working at that time, and got us a reservation. He returned to the rental car counter. The person told him that he did not have a reservation. He asked her to check again. The reservation was there! At this point, we were headed to Chicago, Illinois, for another convention. They had one car left with Illinois plates, which was where we were going! This whole situation testifies that, yes, Jesus was and is my present help in trouble!

Let's pause here and reflect on the 9/11 incident. Our nation will never be the same. My heart goes out to the families that lost their loved ones on that day. My prayers are with you. I also want to take this opportunity to express my gratitude to all of the first responders, firefighters, police officers, and EMTs, as well as the ones serving in our military. I salute you!

As I was previously talking about flying, let's look at an amazing flight still to come. I am looking forward to the Lord Jesus calling His children home, those who have put their faith and trust in Him. In 1 Thessalonians 4:16-17 we are told, "For the Lord Himself will descend from heaven with a shout, with the voice of an archangel, and with the trumpet of God. And the dead in Christ will rise first. Then we who are alive and remain shall be caught up together with them in the clouds to meet the Lord in the air. And thus we shall always be with the Lord."

What a flight that will be! One day, if the Lord allows me to live on this earth and participate in this event, it will be a flight like I have never known.

There are people who think that Disney's rides are thrilling and some are quite breathtaking. However, if you are a born-again Christian, when Jesus calls us home, it will be a flight out of this world! I will fly higher than I have ever flown before. Delta will have nothing on me. I will fly to my Lord and Savior Jesus Christ.

Do you ever look up to the clouds and think of seeing Jesus? I do. The Bible speaks of this in Titus 2:13. "Looking for the blessed hope and glorious appearing of our great God and Savior Jesus Christ."

Can you think of a time like my September 11 ordeal, when He was your present help in trouble? Have you ever thought of how many times, as believers, He has been our present help in trouble and we did not realize it? How many times has He protected us and kept us from evil? Jesus says in Psalm 46:1, "God is our refuge and strength, a very present help in trouble." He knew that we would have trouble. The definition of *refuge* is *a protective haven*. He is our refuge! Is that not encouraging? What a God!

He is our present help in trouble, and He is our peace as well. There are so many people looking for peace. Do you have peace? Let's talk about how to get peace. Jesus wants to be your *Prince of Peace*. If ever we needed peace, it is now.

Have you ever tried to go to sleep at night and your thoughts keep going and going and going? You toss and turn looking at the clock 1 a.m., 3 a.m. and then it's time get up. I have. Did you know that Jesus knows your thoughts, and He also knows when you get up and lay down? Let's read this in Psalm 139:1-2. "O

Lord, You have searched me and known me. You know my sitting down and my rising up; You understand my thought afar of."

There are many things that can steal our peace. For example worrying about our health, about our finances or about the future. However, if you are saved, you have the Prince of Peace living in you through the Holy Spirit. In Galatians 5:22-23 we read, "But the fruit of the Spirit is love, joy, peace, longsuffering, kindness, goodness, faithfulness, gentleness, self-control. Against such there is no law."

We need to allow the Holy Spirit to live His life in and through us. We often keep ourselves from peace because of our lack of faith in God's constant care for us. In Isaiah 26:3 we read, "You will keep *him* in perfect peace, *whose* mind is stayed *on You,* because he trusts in You." We need to look at Jesus and not our circumstances.

Let's read John 14:27. "Peace I leave with you, My peace I give to you; not as the world gives do I give to you. Let not your heart be troubled, neither let it be afraid." The Lord Jesus was very clear in that He left us a gift: peace. From this verse, He knew that there would be times that we would be troubled and afraid.

There are two kinds of peace: peace *with* God and the peace *of* God. In order to have the peace *with* God, you have to accept Jesus Christ as your Lord and Savior. As I mentioned earlier, each of us is separated from God because of sin. Therefore, when a person recognizes that he is a sinner and asks Jesus to forgive him of his sins, realizing that only He can forgive and save them, and accepts His forgiveness – only then, and I reiterate this, only then, can a person have peace *with* God.

A person who is unsaved is a person without peace. This person is unable to find peace anywhere. He may find some contentment, but not a true and lasting peace in their heart. The reason for this is that unsaved people are depending upon themselves. Without Jesus Christ, the Prince of Peace, a person cannot find peace.

The other kind of peace is *of* God. We read about this peace in Philippians 4:7 "And the peace of God, which surpasses all understanding, will guard your hearts and minds through Christ Jesus." It is the peace of God which believers experience when they are leaning upon God.

> Stayed upon Jehovah,
> Hearts are fully blessed;
> Finding, as He promised,
> Perfect peace and rest.
> ~ Frances Ridley Havergal [28]

I believe when a person has peace, he is calm, contented, and relaxed in his spirit. However, when a person does not have peace, he is frustrated, upset, worried – just agitated in general.

When I had melanoma, a suspicious mole, the dermatologist removed it for a biopsy. When the biopsy was performed the mole was shaved off and not cut out.

A t this point the doctor did not know that it was going to be cancer. However, the pathology report came back that it was melanoma. Due to the fact of it being shaved off, my oncologist suggested that I have a sentinel lymph node biopsy performed to rule out that it had spread. Praise the Lord, it came back negative. I will never forget what Heather, my sister-in-law, prayed. She prayed that I would have peace. We need peace.

When we as believers go through health problems, financial difficulties, children issues, or whatever the situation, we need peace. However, there are many people who are looking for peace in all the wrong places:

1. It is not in drugs.

2. It is not in alcohol.

3. It is not in "religions."

4. It is not in suicide.

5. It is not in divorce.

Peace is not found in places or things but in a person, Jesus Christ. In Hannah Whitall Smith's book, *Perfect Peace*, she says, "That deep and lasting peace and comfort of soul, which nothing earthly can disturb, and which is declared to be the portion of those who embrace it, comes only from the Lord Jesus Christ." [29]

What has stolen your peace? Are you focusing on your marriage that you feel may be heading straight for divorce? Does a financial situation look quite dim? Do you have a child that is going the wrong way and you know they are headed for heartache? What about a job that could be gone tomorrow? Are you worrying about having a medical problem and not being able to afford treatment? Are you so upset about the future that you are full of fear?

These questions are real-life questions. If you are like me, you have been concerned at times about your children and the choices that they have made. Let me pause here a moment. If you have never had any biological children and if you have had the privilege to raise stepchildren, count it a blessing. It is a joy! Hopefully, you can take them to church and raise them in the admonition of the Lord (see Ephesians 6:4). I love my stepsons. They are my boys! It can be such a wonderful opportunity with the Lord's help to teach them about Jesus and even lead them to Christ.

Let's return to our discussion of peace in our lives. I remember reading some time ago about a bird in a book. [30] The book was written by Joyce Meyer. She said, "Have you ever seen a bird sitting in a tree having a nervous breakdown? Have you ever seen a bird pacing back and forth saying to himself, 'Oh, I wonder where my next worm is coming from? I need worms! What if God quits making worms today? I don't know what I would do. Maybe I would starve to death!'"

As I have thought about Joyce's words, I have begun to watch birds. They fly, gather their food, chirp – they are not depressed but rather happy. Jesus takes care of them. Let's read in Matthew 6:26, "Look at the birds of the air, for they neither *sow nor reap nor gather into barns; yet your heavenly Father feeds them. Are you not of more* value than they?"

So, after reading this verse, why do we, those of us who have been born again, struggle with anxiety, fear, worry, and depression, when we have a heavenly Father who loves us so much and wants us to have abundant life? How do I know that He wants us to have abundant life? Let's read John 10:10, "The thief does not come except to steal, and to kill, and to destroy. *I have come that they may have life, and that they may have it more abundantly.*"

I think one of Satan's most frequent weapons for those who are saved is fear. Please hear me right. We are to fear God. Let's read this in Leviticus 25:17. "Therefore you shall not oppress one another, but you shall fear your God; for I am the Lord your God."

In my life, I have had fear, but haven't we all? Fear is a horrible emotion. I have experienced times in my life when fear has overtaken me. I guess, over the past several years, the Lord has shown me how to handle fear. It is through Him. When I am afraid, I have tried to remember to speak aloud, "For God has not given us a spirit of fear, but of power and of love and of a sound mind" (2 Timothy 1:7).

Now, let's move on to another issue: our needs. We all have them. Let me clarify this – our needs not our wants. Jesus wants to be our *provider.* Let's read Matthew 6:8. "Therefore do not be like them. For your Father knows the things you have need of before you ask Him." Think about that for a moment. God knows what we need before we ask Him. He knows us.

Also, let's read Philippians 4:19. "And my God shall supply all your need according to His riches in glory by Christ Jesus." Lastly, let's read Psalm 37:25. "I have been young, and *now* am old; yet I have not seen the righteous forsaken, nor his descendants begging bread."

In the book of Exodus, God took care of His people's needs. He delivered them from their enemies, He gave them food, He gave them water to drink, and He guided them. He took care of all their needs.

In Exodus 14, we see how God delivered His people from their enemies by making a way for them to cross the Red Sea.

How many times has He made a way for you to be delivered from your enemies? I remember years ago I had an incident in my life when I received a death threat. I was at a restaurant celebrating my friend's birthday. Rick, who at the time was my fiancé, came into the restaurant pale as a ghost, knelt down beside me, and told me that there had been a death threat on my life.

The Tennessee FBI was called in for the investigation. The threat came in the form of a letter which involved hiring a professional killer and throwing battery acid on me. They believed it to be someone who was working with me. During this time, I was very dependent upon the Lord for keeping me safe. I walked in and out of the company building in the mornings and evenings very cautiously. If this was the person whom the FBI had under suspicion, this person had been in and out of a mental institution. The Lord took care of me and He delivered me from my enemy.

Let's return to Exodus 16. We see that the Lord provided manna for them to eat. How many times has He feed you and is still feeding you? We are so blessed in the United States with great food!

We read in Exodus 17 that God gave them water to drink. God has blessed us as well with great water and ice tea – Southern style, which is my favorite.

Also, we read in Exodus 13: 21-22 that God guided them. He went before them by day in a pillar of cloud to lead the way and by night in a pillar of fire to give them light, as to go by day and night. He has given the Holy Spirit, as well as the Bible, to guide us today.

Through the ages, He has proven Himself to provide for His people. "And my God shall supply all your need according to His riches in glory by Christ Jesus" (Philippians 4:19). He is our provider! Look at that verse again, "And my God shall supply all your need . . ." How much of your need will He supply? All of your needs, not just some, all!

### *"WHERE DID JESUS CHRIST COME FROM?"*

In John 1:1-3 the Bible states, "In the beginning was the Word, and the Word was with God, And the Word was God. He was in the beginning with God. All things were made through Him, and without Him nothing was made that was made."

If you will notice *the Word* was already present in the beginning. You may ask, where does this mention Jesus? Jesus Christ is *the Word*. Jesus Christ was and is a real person. He is not an idea or make-believe. He is as real as you and I.

John begins his Gospel by speaking about *the Word*, but he does not explain at first who or what the Word is. A word is a unit of speech by which we express ourselves to others. But John is not writing about *speech* but rather about a *person*. [31] The person that John is referring to is the Lord Jesus Christ, the Son of God. In addition, we see in Revelation 19:13, "He *was* clothed with a robe dipped in blood, and His name is called Word of God." From this verse, we can clearly see that one of the names for Jesus is the "Word of God."

Furthermore, we read in 1 John 1:1 that Christ was present in the beginning. Likewise, in 1 Peter 1:20, we read, "He indeed was foreordained before the foundation of the world, but was manifest in these last times for you." Christ is an eternal person. What does the word "eternal" mean? Webster's Dictionary defines it as "without end or permanent."

Some words that are used to describe eternity are "endless time," "everlasting," and "forever." Before we go any further, I would like to explain to you the Godhead or the Trinity. The Godhead or the Trinity is three individual persons: God the Father, God the Son, and God the Holy Spirit. The second person is Jesus Christ, who is God's Son.

Jesus clearly states that He was with the Father before the world was created. This is confirmed in John 17:5. "And now, O Father, glorify Me together with Yourself, with the glory which I had with You before the world was." We can conclude from this verse that Christ was with the Father before the world was created. Therefore, His birth on this earth was not His beginning.

Let's read John 6:62. "*What* then if you should see the Son of Man ascend where He was before?" So, this verse tells us that, "He was before . . ." We know He pre-existed because in Genesis 1:1 it states, "In the beginning God created the heavens and the earth." Therefore, He had to have existed prior to the creation in order to create it.

Let me emphasize this through John 1:1-3. "In the beginning was the Word, and the Word was with God, and the Word was God. He was in the beginning with God. All things were made through Him, and without Him nothing was made that was made." Once again, these verses confirm that Jesus was with God in the beginning before the earth was created.

Some people may wonder why the doctrine of the pre-existence of Jesus is so important. The doctrine is the foundational structure on which the Christian faith is built. For you see, if Christ did not pre-exist, then He would not be eternal.

Therefore, the eternal Trinity – God the Father, God the Son and God the Holy Spirit – would not exist. Also, if Christ is not eternal, then He cannot be God. That leads us to the conclusion that if He is not God, then He is not the creator and redeemer. Christ's pre-existence is of upmost importance to His deity, which means He is God.

The doctrine of Jesus Christ's pre-existence is also seen in John 17:5. "And now, O Father, glorify Me together with Yourself, with the glory which I had with You before the world was."

We see Jesus in each of the sixty-six books of the Bible:

1. Genesis – He is the creator God.

2. Exodus – He is our redeemer.

3. Leviticus – He is our sanctification.

4. Numbers – He is our guide.

5. Deuteronomy – He is our teacher.

6. Joshua – He is our mighty conqueror.

7. Judges – He gives victory over our enemies.

8. Ruth – He is our kinsman, our lover, and our redeemer.

9. 1 Samuel – He is the root of Jesse.

10. 2 Samuel – He is the son of David.

11. 1 Kings – He is the king of kings.

12. 2 Kings – He is the Lord of Lords.

13. 1 Chronicles – He is our intercessor.

14. 2 Chronicles – He is our high priest.

15. Ezra – He is the temple and the house of worship.

16. Nehemiah – He is our mighty wall, protecting us from our enemies.

17. Esther – He stands in the gap to deliver us from our enemies.

18. Job – He is the arbitrator who not only understands our struggles, but also has the power to do something about them.

19. Psalms – He is our song and our reason to sing.

20. Proverbs – He is our wisdom, helping us to make sense of life and live it successfully.

21. Ecclesiastes – He is our purpose, delivering us from vanity.

22. Song of Solomon – He loves us, our Rose of Sharon.

23. Isaiah – He is our mighty counselor, our Prince of Peace, our everlasting Father and more. He is everything we need.

24. Jeremiah – He is our balm of Gilead, the soothing salve for our sin-sick soul.

25. Lamentations – He is the ever-faithful One upon whom we can depend.

26. Ezekiel – He is our wheel in the middle of a wheel the One who assures that dry, dead bones will come alive again.

27. Daniel – He is the ancient of days, our everlasting God who never runs out of time.

28. Hosea – He is our faithful Lover, always beckoning us to come back, even when we have abandoned Him.

29. Joel – He is our refuge, keeping us safe in times of trouble.

30. Amos – He is our husbandman, the One you can depend on to stay by your side.

31. Obadiah – He is the Lord of the Kingdom.

32. Jonah – He is our salvation, bringing us back within His will.

33. Micah – He is judge of the nation.

34. Nahum – He is the jealous God.

35. Habakkuk – He is the Holy One.

36. Zephaniah – He is the witness.

37. Haggai – He overthrows our enemies.

38. Zechariah – He is our Lord of hosts.

39. Malachi – He is the sun of righteousness with healing in His wings.

40. Matthew – He is king of the Jews.

41. Mark – He is the servant.

42. Luke – He is the son of man, feeling what we feel.

43. John – He is the Son of God.

44. Acts – He is the savior of the world.

45. Romans – He is the righteousness of God.

46. 1 Corinthians – He is the rock that followed Israel.

47. 2 Corinthians – He is the triumphant One, giving victory.

48. Galatians – He is our liberty; He sets us free.

49. Ephesians – He is the head of the church, which is His body.

50. Philippians – He is our joy.

51. Colossians – He is our completeness.

52. 1 Thessalonians – He is our hope.

53. 2 Thessalonians – He is our glory.

54. 1 Timothy – He is our faith.

55. 2 Timothy – He is our stability.

56. Titus – He is our faithful pastor.

57. Philemon – He is our benefactor.

58. Hebrews – He is our perfection.

59. James – He is the power behind our faith.

60. 1 Peter – He is our example.

61. 2 Peter – He is our purity.

62. 1 John – He is our life.

63. 2 John – He is our pattern.

64. 3 John – He is our motivation.

65. Jude – He is the foundation of our faith.

66. Revelation – He is our coming king. Praise His name!

So, as you can see Jesus is a believer's everything!

### *"HAS JESUS CHRIST ALWAYS BEEN?"*

The answer is a resounding "yes." In lieu of this fact, it is of upmost importance, as I mentioned earlier, that we examine His pre-existence. It is vital that we keep in mind that when Jesus Christ was born on earth, it was not the beginning of His life. Let's read Genesis 1:1. "In the beginning God created the heavens and the earth." Jesus has always been.

Let's read Colossians 1:15. "He is the image of the invisible God, the firstborn over all creation." Let's pause here for a moment. He is the image of the invisible God. The pre-existent Christ is the express image of the invisible God.

As we continue in verse 15, we see that He is the firstborn over all creation. "Firstborn" denotes two things of Christ: He preceded the whole Creation, and He is Sovereign over all Creation.[32]

Let's also read Hebrews 1:2. "Has in these last days spoken to us by His Son, whom He has appointed heir of all things, through whom also He made the worlds." This verse denotes that Christ pre-existed prior to the universe being created. Let's read John 8:58. "Jesus said to them, 'Most assuredly, I say to you, before Abraham was, I am.'"

## *"WILL JESUS CHRIST ALWAYS BE?"*

Absolutely yes! This is confirmed in Hebrews 13:8. "Jesus Christ is the same yesterday, today, and forever." He will "forever be." The questions that I have for you are: "Do you know Him as your Lord and Savior?" and "Will you be with Him forever throughout eternity?"

In Revelation 4:8, it says, " . . . Who was and is and is to come!" He has always been and always will be. He is eternal. In Revelation 22:5, we read, "There shall be no night there: They need no lamp nor light of the sun, for the Lord God gives them light. And they shall reign forever and ever."

# CHAPTER 2

## *JESUS CHRIST: THE PERFECT GOD-MAN*

I am sure that some of you have asked, "How can Jesus Christ be perfectly God and perfectly Man?" We are going to study this question in depth. The expressions "Son of God" and "Son of Man" are two of the most important descriptions of Christ in the Scriptures. "Son of God" shows that He is the *Son who is related to God.* "Son of Man" shows that He is the *Son who is related to mankind.* Both descriptions dominate the four Gospels – Matthew, Mark, Luke and John.[33]

So, get ready for the most exciting and wonderful time as we encounter the perfect God-Man – Jesus Christ. I get so excited just thinking about Him. He is such an awesome person! I hope and pray that when we finish this chapter that if you do not already feel the way that I do about Him you will.

## *JESUS IS GOD*

As we've discussed, Jesus is the second person of the Trinity. He is God the Son. Christ was truly and perfectly God. The "Son of God" points to the deity of Christ. The word "deity" comes from a Latin word, "Deus," which means "God." When we say that we believe in the "Deity of Christ," we are saying, "I believe that Jesus Christ is God."

It saddens me to learn that many religions maintain that Jesus is not God since the Bible clearly states that He is. This is one of the several verses that confirm that Jesus is the Son of God. In 1 John 5:20 we read, "And we know that the Son of God has come and has given us an understanding, that we may know Him who is true; and we are in Him who is true, in His Son Jesus Christ. This is the true God and eternal life."

Jesus Christ, the Son of God, has the attributes of God. He is *omniscient, omnipresent, omnipotent* and *unchangeable.*

Jesus is *omniscient*, which means *He knows all things*. As John 16:30 says, "Now we are sure that You know all things, and have no need that anyone should question You. By this we believe that You came forth from God."

There are several events in the Bible where Jesus reveals things unknown about Himself as well as other people. We see that Jesus, unlike normal man, foretold His death and resurrection. In Matthew 16:21, we read, "From that time Jesus began to show to His disciples that He must go to Jerusalem, and suffer many things from the elders and chief priests and scribes and be killed, and be raised the third day." Jesus was predicting to His disciples His death and resurrection. This prophecy is repeated in Matthew 20:19.

Also, we read the account of Jesus knowing that a coin is in a fish's mouth before the fish is even caught! "Nevertheless, lest we offend them, go to the sea, cast in a hook, and take the fish that comes up first. And when you have opened its mouth, you will find a piece of money; take that and give it them for Me and you" (Matthew 17:27). Imagine that! He is an amazing God! In addition, we read in John 4:1-26 about a Samaritan woman who meets Jesus. Let's read verses 16-19 of this story. "Jesus said to her, 'Go, call your husband, and come here.' The woman answered and said, 'I have no husband.' Jesus said to her, 'You have well said, I have no husband,' 'for you have had five husbands, and the one whom you now have is not your husband; in that you spoke truly.' The woman said to Him, 'Sir, I perceive that You are a prophet.'" Notice that Jesus had never met this woman before. Nevertheless, He knew how many husbands she had been married to. Let's read verse 29 of this chapter. "Come, see a Man who told me all things that I ever did. Could this be the Christ?" Jesus knows all things.

Jesus is *omnipresent*, which means *He is always and everywhere present*. "For where two or three are gathered together in My name, I am there in the midst of them" (Matthew 18:20). Let's also read Matthew 28:20. "Teaching them to observe all things that I have commanded you; and lo, I am with you always, *even* to the end of the age. Amen."

Jesus is *omnipotent*, which means *He is Almighty and All-powerful*. Let's read Revelation 1:8 where He is seen as the Almighty. "'I am the Alpha and the Omega, *the* Beginning and *the* End,' says the Lord, 'who is and who was and who is to come, the Almighty.'" In Matthew 28:18, we see Him as all-powerful. "And Jesus came and spoke to them, saying, 'All authority has been given to Me in heaven and on earth.'" Jesus is *unchangeable*, which means *He never changes*. "Jesus Christ *is* the same yesterday, today and forever" (Hebrews 13:8). He is, was, and will always be the same.

Much like an attorney who already has proved his case beyond a reasonable doubt, our Lord adds the audible testimony of God the Father to the awesome accumulated evidence of who Jesus really is. We know of three times during the life of Christ that God Himself spoke from heaven to verify the identity of His Son.[34] These are:

(1) The voice of God at the baptism of Jesus (Matthew 3:16-17).

(2) The voice of God at the transfiguration (Matthew 17:5).

(3) The voice of God four days before the crucifixion (John 12:28-33).

These three verses confirm that Jesus is God. He is the living Son of the most high God. He is not on a cross. He is alive and seated on the right hand of God the Father at this very moment (Ephesians 1:20).

## *JESUS IS MAN*

Jesus became God in the flesh because of His sinless nature. You may ask, "What was the purpose of Jesus, leaving heaven and coming to earth, in the form of a man?" Or another way to ask this question is "Why did God, through Jesus, become flesh?" To answer this question, let's return to the garden of Eden, which we find in the book of Genesis.

Genesis is the first book of the Bible, and the Greek word "Genesis" means "origin, generation, or beginning." In Henry Morris' book, *The Genesis Record*, he states, "It has often been pointed out that if a person really believes Genesis 1:1, he will not find it difficult to believe anything else recorded in the Bible." That is, if God really created all things, then He controls all things and can do all things.[35]

Genesis begins with the creation of the earth as well as the creation of mankind and it provides a solid framework for understanding the big picture of the Bible. The author of Genesis is believed to be Moses. This book of beginnings introduces us to God and His holiness, righteousness, grace and mercy. It also introduces us to His creation, man's sin, and God's plan of redemption as it began to unfold through Abraham and his descendants.[36] Most of the books of the Bible draw on the contents of Genesis in one way or another.

Some people believe that Adam and Eve in Genesis are fictional. However, they were real people, just as real as you and me. If they had not been real, then they would not have committed a real sin and in that case, Jesus would not have had to die. Remember: He chose to die to pay for the sins of the world. (See 1 John 2:2.)

You may wonder how Adam and Eve relate to Jesus Christ coming to this earth as a man. This is why we are beginning in Genesis 1:1. "In the beginning God created the heavens and the earth." God took six days for creation and rested on the seventh day. Let's look at what He created on these six days:

1st Day:   *God made light.* The light He called day and the darkness He called night (Genesis 1:3-5).

2nd Day:   *God made the sky, which He called heaven* (Genesis 1:6-8).

3rd Day:   *God made the seas and the dry land.* The land He called *earth.* Also, He made plants of every kind (Genesis 1:9-13).

4th Day:   *God made the sun for the day and the moon for the night. He also made the stars* (Genesis 1:14-19).

5th Day:   *God made fish and other creatures of the sea. He made the birds of the air* (Genesis 1:20-23).

6th Day:   *God made animals of the land. He also created one man—Adam* (Genesis 1:24-30). In Genesis 1:31 we read, *"Then God saw everything that He had made, and indeed it was very good . . ."*

7th Day:   *He rested.* In Genesis 2:3, "Then God blessed the seventh day and sanctified it, because in it He rested from all His work which God had created and made."

Can you just imagine a world where everything was in order? A world that had no suffering, no pain, no sin, and no death? Our world today is so out of order. It is full of crime, suffering, disease, terrorism, and war. It is evil.

A person used to be able to go to the shopping mall and not have to worry about being mugged. It used to be you could send your child to school and not have to worry about shootings. It used to be you could sit down and watch a "clean" movie and not have to worry about nudity and violence.

It used to be that the American people took abortion seriously; instead, approximately 3,700 are performed each day and 1.37 million each year in the United States. The count per day worldwide is approximately 115,000. The number per year worldwide is approximately forty-two million.

It used to be that we could go to church and not have to worry about someone coming in and opening fire on us. We live in a depraved society. Let's return to Genesis. We have seen so far that God created the heaven, the earth, the creatures and mankind. He is the Creator of all. We read this in Colossians 1:16. "For by Him all things were created that are in heaven and that are on earth, visible and invisible, whether thrones or dominions or principalities or powers. All things were created through Him and for Him."

Have you ever wondered why you were created? To find the answer, let's look at the end of Colossians 1:16 ". . . for Him." You were created for Him. When I go to the mall, I see "It's all about me" quotes, whether it is clothing, songs, or books. However, it is not all about us. It is all about Him! You are here because the Lord allows you to be here.

A person was not created to be a robot. He or she is a free agent with a moral ability to love Jesus or reject Jesus. However, a person cannot be saved without the Father drawing them to Him. In John 6:46 we read, "Not that anyone has seen the Father, except He who is from God; He has seen the Father." A person left on his or her own does not seek after God. "There is none who understands; There is none who seeks after God" (Romans 3:11).

Since we are looking at being created, let's return to Adam in Genesis. We know that God created Adam. "And the Lord

God formed man of the dust of the ground, and breathed into his nostrils the breath of life; and became a living being" (Genesis 2:7).

Let's see where God put this man that He had created. Let's read Genesis 2:8. "The Lord God planted a garden eastward in Eden, and there He put the man whom He had formed." Why do you think that God put Adam in the garden of Eden? Let's read Genesis 2:15 and find the answer. "Then the Lord God took the man and put him in the garden of Eden to tend and keep it." God put Adam there to take care of the garden.

Let's continue reading in Genesis 2:16-17 and see what the Lord God commanded the man. "And the Lord God commanded the man, saying, 'Of every tree of the garden you may freely eat; but of the tree of the knowledge of good and evil you shall not eat, for in the day that you eat of it you shall surely die.'" What did God tell him would happen if he ate of the tree of the knowledge of good and evil? He told him that if he ate from the tree he would *surely die.* Not *maybe* he would die he would *surely* die.

Let's pause a moment and factor in a characteristic of God. God cannot lie. Let's read this in Hebrews 6:18. "That by two immutable things, in which it is impossible for God to lie, we might have strong consolation, who have fled for refuge to lay hold of the hope set before us." Therefore, when God said that if he ate from the tree of the knowledge of good and evil, he would surely die *that means that he would surely die.*

Let's see how Eve is created. We read in Genesis 2:21-23, "And the Lord God caused a deep sleep to fall on Adam, and he slept; and He took one of his ribs, and closed up the flesh in its place. *Then the rib which the Lord God had taken from man He made a woman,* and He brought her to the man. And Adam said, 'This is now bone of my bones and flesh of my flesh; *she shall be called Woman, because she was taken out of Man.*'"

Now, we have Adam and Eve living in the garden of Eden. They were living in a perfect environment. At this point, Adam and Eve lived in a world that was in order, if you will. It had no pain, no suffering, no disease, no death and absolutely no sin. Their lives were perfect.

They did not have to worry about doctor appointments, family struggles, financial difficulties, crime, wars, earthquakes, terrorism – they lived in a perfect environment. In Genesis 1:31 it states, "Then God saw everything that He had made, and indeed it was very good . . . ." It was *very good*, not just good, but *very good*.

However, in Chapter 3 of Genesis, their lives change forever. Let's read Genesis 3:1-3. "Now the serpent was more cunning than any beast of the field which the Lord God had made. And he said to the woman, 'Has God indeed said', 'You shall not eat of every tree of the garden?' And the woman said to the serpent, 'We may eat the fruit of the trees of the garden; but of the fruit of the tree which is in the midst of the garden, God has said, 'You shall not eat it, nor shall you touch it, lest you die.'"

Notice that Eve added to what God had told them. In verse 3, " . . . nor shall you touch it, lest you die." God told them in Genesis 2:17, "But of the tree of the knowledge of good and evil you shall not eat, for in the day that you eat of it you shall surely die."

Eve said that God told them that if they eat it or touch the fruit, they would die. God told them not to *eat* from the tree of the knowledge of good and evil.

In Genesis 3:6 we read, "So when the woman saw that the tree was good for food, that it was pleasant to the eyes, and a tree desirable to make one wise, she took of its fruit and ate. She also gave to her husband with her, and he ate." At this point, they have disobeyed God.

Let's keep reading in Genesis with verse 7. "Then the eyes of both of them were opened, and they knew that they were naked; and they sewed fig leaves together and made themselves coverings."

Let's see what happens next. In Genesis 3:8, we read, "And they heard the sound of the *Lord God walking in the garden in the cool of the day,* and Adam and his wife hid themselves from the presence of the Lord God among the trees of the garden."

When I read this, I love that the Lord God was walking in the garden in the cool of the day. Can you imagine? The Lord God was walking in the garden.

We have a riverpark in Chattanooga that is for walkers and anyone else who enjoys the outdoors. It is so beautiful. The Tennessee River flows along the walkway, and there are trees on either side. It is just beautiful. I walk there frequently.

In the mornings the dew is on the ground, the water is sparkling, the chipmunks and squirrels are running around, and the birds are chirping. It is so peaceful, so calming and, again, so beautiful. It makes me think of the garden of Eden. How do you imagine the garden of Eden?

What if the Lord God walked at our riverpark in the cool of the day? Wouldn't that be awesome? I have spent time while I walk talking to the Lord. You know, He may not be there in a physical body; but since I am saved, He is with me in Spirit. I am sealed with the Holy Spirit. If you are saved, you are as well.

We read this in Ephesians 1:13-14. "In Him you also trusted, after you heard the word of truth, the gospel of your salvation; in whom also, having believed, you were sealed with the Holy Spirit of promise, who is the guarantee of our inheritance until the redemption of the purchased possession, to the praise of His glory."

Why do you suppose that God was walking in the garden of Eden? I believe that He wanted to have closeness, intimacy and communion with Adam and Eve. God is so personal. He loves to have fellowship with us. He loves us.

Let that resonate in your heart and mind. He, the God of the Universe, loves us and loves spending time with us. He is even preparing for us an eternal home to spend with Him throughout eternity (see John 14:2-3). That is, those of us who have accepted Jesus, His Son, as our Lord and Savior.

In Genesis 3: 9-14 we read, "Then the Lord God called to Adam and said to him, 'Where are you?' So he said, 'I heard Your voice in the garden, and I was afraid because I was naked; and I hid myself.' And He said, 'Who told you that you were naked? Have you eaten from the tree of which I commanded you that you should not eat?' Then the man said, 'The woman whom you gave to be with me, she gave me of the tree, and I ate.' And the Lord God said to the woman, 'What is this you have done?' The woman said, 'The serpent deceived me, and I ate.'"

Have you ever considered the fact that when God asked Adam and Eve if they had eaten from the tree that He commanded them not to eat from, they could have confessed their sin and asked for forgiveness? But, they did not.

When God tells us not to do something and we disobey Him and do it anyway, knowing that we have sinned, what do we do? Do we think that we can get away from God by hiding our sin? Do we cover it up? Do we blame others? Let's see what the Bible tells us to do when we sin. Let's read 1 John 1:9. "If we confess our sins, He is faithful and just to forgive us our sins and to cleanse us from all unrighteousness."

On the other hand, what happens if we try to hide our sins? Let's read Proverbs 28:13. "He who covers his sins will not prosper, but whoever confesses and forsakes them will have mercy."

Let's see what happened to King David when he did not confess his sin to the Lord. In Psalm 32:3-5 we read, "When I kept silent, my bones grew old through my groaning all the day long. For day and night Your hand was heavy upon me; my vitality was turned into the drought of summer. I acknowledged my sin to You, and my iniquity I have not hidden. I said, 'I will confess my transgressions to the Lord' – and You forgave the iniquity of my sin."

The psalmist experienced forgiveness when he acknowledged his sin, but it came only after divine chastening. When he was silent and did not confess his sin, he was weakened physically and grieved inwardly. The hand (or power) of the Lord was heavy on him (Psalm 32:4) that is, God dealt severely with him. The result was that his vitality (strength) was sapped (or dried up) as in the summer heat. This expression may refer to physical illness with burning fever, or it may describe in poetic language his remorse of conscience. Therefore, he confessed his sin to God. This is the way of restoration, for God forgave him. [37]

One particular sin that I committed years ago stands out. I went to a department store and was standing in line to purchase a pair of pants and other items. When I got to the counter, the sales clerk did not ring up the pants. I thought I just got a free pair of pants. So, I left and went home.

Throughout the week, the Holy Spirit kept telling me to make it right. Therefore, I went back to the department store. I went to customer service and handed them the pants. I told them that I was a Christian and that the sales clerk failed to charge me for them. I turned around and walked out. I felt that a load had been lifted off of me. I'm sure that the customer service people did not know what to think.

When you are a Christian, the Holy Spirit will convict you immediately about sin. Praise the Lord for that conviction! If you do not have that conviction on your life when you sin, check and see if you are truly born again!

Let's return to Adam and Eve. As I mentioned earlier in this chapter, prior to Adam and Eve's disobedience, they lived in a perfect and sinless environment. However, when they disobeyed God and ate of the tree of the knowledge of good and evil, their lives changed.

Let's see what God does next. In Genesis 3:21 we read, "Also for Adam and his wife the Lord God made tunics of skin, and clothed them." These tunics of skin were provided by God through the death of an animal. This pictures the robe of righteousness which is provided for guilty sinners through the shed blood of the Lamb of God, made available to us on the basis of faith.[38]

Let's return to Genesis 3:9. "Then the Lord God called to Adam and said to him, 'Where are you?'" This question proves two things – that man was lost and that God had come to seek. It proves man's sin and God's grace.[39]

What were the coverings that Adam and Eve made? Let's read Genesis 3:7 to find out. "Then the eyes of both of them were opened, and they knew that they were naked; and they sewed fig leaves together, and made themselves coverings." The aprons of fig leaves speak of man's attempt to save himself by a bloodless religion of good works.[40]

A person cannot save herself or himself. Why? Let's read Isaiah 64:6. "But we are all like an unclean thing, and all our righteousnesses are like filthy rages; we all fade as a leaf, and our iniquities, like the wind, have taken us away." We are *all* unclean!

However, here is the good news. When we call upon Jesus to forgive us of our sins, His blood covers us and we are *justified* in His sight. You may be wondering what "justified" or "justification" mean. *They mean the process by which sinful human beings are made acceptable to a Holy God.* Christianity is unique because of its teaching of justification by grace (see Romans 3:24).

*Justification is God's declaration that the demands of His Law have been fulfilled in the righteousness of His Son.* The basis for this justification is the death of Christ. Justification is based on the work of Christ, accomplished through His blood (see Romans 5:9) and brought to His people through His resurrection (see Romans 4:25).[41]

When God justifies, He charges the sin of man to Christ and credits the righteousness of Christ to the believer (see 2 Corinthians 5:21). The negative result of justification is what we are *saved from:* " . . . having now been justified by His blood, we shall be saved from wrath through Him" (Romans 5:9). The positive result is what we are *saved to:* " . . . whom He called, these He also justified; and whom He justified, these He also glorified" (Romans 8:30).

The Apostle Paul, in Romans 5:1, states, "Therefore, having been justified by faith, we have peace with God through our Lord Jesus Christ." We, as believers in Christ, have peace with God.

God slew innocent animals. At the price of the blood of those animals, He made coats for Adam and Eve. Thus, we have the first blood covering, and since that day when God covered Adam and Eve at the price of the shed blood of the innocent animals, there has been no covering *apart* from the blood of the innocent sacrifice of the Lamb of God.[42] *Rivers* of blood flowed from Genesis to Malachi. Tens of thousands of animals, doves, and pigeons were slain and their blood was offered on the altar.[43]

Let's also read Hebrews 10:1-6. "For the law, having a shadow of the good things to come, and not the very image of the things, can never with these same sacrifices, which they offer continually year by year, make those who approach perfect. For then would they not have ceased to be offered? For the worshipers, once purified, would have had no more consciousness of sins. But in those sacrifices there is a reminder of sins every year. For it is not possible that the blood of bulls and goats could take away sins. Therefore, when He came into the world, He said: 'Sacrifice and offering You did not desire, but a body You have prepared for Me. In burnt offerings and sacrifices for sin You had no pleasure.'"

Friend, every innocent animal slain in the Old Testament era pointed to the blood of the Lamb of God, foreordained before the foundation of the world. His blood, shed on Calvary, made good the offerings of those in the Old Testament who, in faith, offered blood on the altar. If Jesus had not died on the cross, the blood shed throughout the Old Testament era would have been shed in vain, and those who offered it would have died without hope and their spirits would be tormented in the pits of the damned![44]

For you see, it was through Adam and Eve's sin that sin entered into the world. We see confirmation of this in Romans 5:12. "Therefore, just as through one man sin entered the world, and death through sin, and thus death spread to all men, because all sinned . . ." Also, in 1 Corinthians 15:22 we read, "For as in Adam all die, even so in Christ all shall be made alive." Accordingly, sin begins in Genesis but ends in Revelation. In Revelation 22:3, it states, "And there shall be no more curse, but the throne of God and of the Lamb shall be in it, and His servants shall serve Him." In heaven, there will be no more sin.

Thus, the curse of Adam's sin led to death for everyone. Therefore, in order to save mankind, we had to have a perfect Man to die on the cross for imperfect people. Jesus Christ is the "Perfect Lamb of God without blemish and without spot."

"But with the precious blood of Christ, as of a lamb without blemish and without spot. He indeed was foreordained before the foundation of the world, but was manifest in these last times for you" (1 Peter 1:19-20).

Let's read Hebrews 9:22. "And according to the law almost all things are purified with blood, and without shedding of blood there is not remission." Jesus was the ultimate sacrifice to restore mankind back to God. Remember in the Old Testament that animal sacrifices were required for sins.

Let's read Hebrews 10:3-4. "But in those *sacrifices there is* a reminder of sins every year. For *it is* not possible that the blood of bulls and goats could take away sins." Also, we read in

Hebrews 10:11-12, "And every priest stands ministering daily and offering repeatedly the same sacrifices, which can never take away sins. But this Man, after He had offered one sacrifice for sins forever, sat down at the right hand of God."

When Jesus came as a man to this earth, He came to save the lost people. "For the Son of Man has come to save that which was lost" (Matthew 18:11). We also read in Matthew 9:13, " . . . For I did not come to call the righteous, but sinners, to repentance."

Before a person is born again, he or she is dead in their sins or spiritually dead. Because when Adam and Eve sinned, we sinned. Therefore, we are separated from God. We are all born spiritually dead. You may be wondering what *spiritually dead* means. Prior to accepting Jesus Christ as Lord and Savior, a person is dead spiritually, separated from a relationship with God the Father because of sin.

Let's read Ephesians 2:5. "Even when we were dead in trespasses, made us alive together with Christ (by grace you have been saved)."

Let's take a moment to talk about *grace*. What is grace? Grace can be defined as *God's undeserved, unearned favor, goodness, kindness, and love toward us.* God's grace is mentioned 150 times in the New Testament. It has been said that G-R-A-C-E is "God's Riches At Christ's Expense." Our sin-debt was paid in full through Jesus' death on the cross. We have the privilege of coming to His throne with all our requests. *Mercy* is "*not getting what we deserve,*" namely, punishment for our sins. *Grace* is "*getting what we don't deserve,*" that is, *favor from God.*[45]

The only way to have a relationship with God the Father is through His Son, Jesus Christ. In John 14:6, we read, "Jesus said to him, 'I am *The Way, The Truth* and *The Life.* No one comes to the Father except through Me.'" Notice that Jesus said, " . . . I am *The Way* . . ." He did not say a way or one of the ways. He said "*The Way.*" Also in this verse, " . . . No one comes to the Father except though Me." So, how many people can go to the Father without going though Jesus, His Son? No one. This verse is crystal clear.

We must realize God is a holy God, as well as a perfect God. In Revelation 4:6-8 we read, "Before the throne there was a sea of glass, like crystal. And in the midst of the throne, and around the throne, were four living creatures full of eyes in front and in back. The first living creature was like a lion, the second living creature was like a calf, the third living creature had a face like a man, and the fourth living creature was like a flying eagle. The four living creatures, each having six wings, were full of eyes around and within. And they do not rest day or night, saying: *'Holy, holy, holy, Lord God Almighty, Who was and is and is to come!'*"

Think about these verses. "And they do not rest day or night, saying: 'Holy, holy, holy, Lord God Almighty, Who was and is and is to come!'" As I write this, they are saying, "Holy, holy, holy, Lord God Almighty, Who was and is and is to come!" The Lord God Almighty is holy! We also read in Revelation 15:4, "Who shall not fear You, O Lord, and glorify Your name? For *You alone are holy.*" He is holy! So, how does a sinner make peace with a Holy God? The only way a sinner can make peace with a Holy God is through His Son, Jesus Christ.

In Romans 3:23 it states, "For all have sinned and fall short of the glory of God." You may ask, "What does this mean?" We have all sinned, because of Adam's sin, whether you are a Jew or Gentile, we are all sinners. Not only have we sinned, but we have fallen short of the glory of God. If you look at the verb usage, *fall short* can be translated *keep on falling short.*

This is where people, who are under the assumption that by their own efforts they will go to heaven, need to realize that they will never measure up to the glory of God. What does it mean *to fall short of the glory of God? It is a failure to meet divine standard*. When measured by God's standards of perfection, which means being perfect, we fail or miss the mark.

For example, my family loves going to Disney World in Florida. At Disney, if you have a child, there are certain rides that require that your child be a certain height in order to ride it. There were a few years that our sons did not meet the height restrictions. They missed the mark. Therefore, they missed the ride. Likewise, we miss the mark of God's standards, because He is perfect and He expects perfection. We are not perfect, so we miss the mark.

Have you ever thought about what it means to be perfect? When Jesus was on the earth, He was perfect. He was a perfect baby. A perfect child. A perfect teenager and a perfect adult! He was flesh and blood –a human – who never sinned.

He did not think evil thoughts toward people who hurt Him. On the contrary, let's read what He did. "Then Jesus said, 'Father, forgive them, for they do not know what they do.' And they divided His garments and cast lots" (Luke 23:34). He did not gossip about people. He did not lie. He did not steal. In 1 Peter 2:22 we read, "Who committed no sin, nor was deceit found in His mouth." He was and is perfect in all ways!

Can you just imagine the disciples spending time with Jesus, who was and is perfect? As we have previously discussed, He was physically a man. He ate and slept as we do – but He was perfect. When we look at Jesus and we look at ourselves, we see how much we miss the mark. How imperfect we are! What sinners we are! We need a savior and praise God we have one – Jesus Christ the one and only savior of the world!

You may ask, "Why did Jesus come to this earth, live here and then He was killed?" Well to begin with, we have talked about God creating the earth and man perfect. However, when Adam and Eve sinned and disobeyed God's commands, He had to punish them. If God, who is just, overlooked sin, it would make Him unjust. God's punishment for sin is death.

Let's read Romans 6:23. "For the wages of sin is death, but the gift of God is eternal life in Christ Jesus our Lord."

When Adam sinned, every human being became guilty of disobeying God's laws. "Therefore, just as through one man sin entered the world, and death through sin, and thus death spread to all men, because all sinned . . ." (Romans 5:12).

Now, let's read in Genesis 3:15 of a great promise. "And I will put enmity between you and the woman, and between your seed and her Seed; He shall bruise your head, and you shall bruise His heel." This promise has long been known as the *Protevangelium*, which means *The First Gospel*. It predicts the perpetual hostility between Satan and the woman (representing all mankind) and between Satan's seed (his agents) and her Seed (the Messiah, who is Jesus).[46]

The woman's seed would crush the Devil's head, a mortal wound spelling utter defeat. This wound was administered at Calvary when the Lord and Savior Jesus Christ decisively triumphed over the Devil. Satan, in turn, would bruise the Messiah's heel. The heel wound here speaks of suffering and even of physical death, but not of ultimate defeat. Therefore, Christ suffered on the cross, and even died, but He arose from the dead, victorious over sin, hell and Satan. [47]

"For even the Son of Man did not come to be served, but to serve, and to give His life a ransom for many" (Mark 10:45). It is clearly indicated that Jesus needed to become a man in order to die for the sins of mankind.

There are a number of reasons why God became man,[48] through Jesus:

1. To confirm God's promises – He became man in order to confirm the promises made to the fathers and to show mercy to the Gentiles (see Romans 15:8-12). Beginning with the promise in Genesis 3:15 and continuing through the Old Testament, God at various times promised to send his Son into the world.

2. To reveal the Father – In the Old Testament, God is revealed as creator and governor. The Old Testament reveals the unity, holiness, might, and beneficence of God. Christ completed the revelation by adding the idea of God as Father (see Matthew 6:9). The relationship of the child of God to his heavenly Father is a precious New Testament concept.

3. To become a faithful high priest – He came in order to become qualified to act as the faithful high priest. You may ask why this is important. If you recall, in Leviticus, the people had to go to the high priest and seek atonement for their sins. These priests had certain tasks, and one of them was pronouncement of forgiveness of sins. God set these priests apart to be the mediator between Him and man. God did not deal directly with sinful people, because He is holy. Rather, He had the priests to fulfill this purpose.

4. To put away sin – He came to put away sin by the sacrifice of Himself.

5. To destroy the works of the devil – "He who sins is of the devil, for the devil has sinned from the beginning. For this purpose the Son of God was manifested, that He might destroy the works of the devil" (1 John 3:8). When Christ came, especially with His work on the cross, He brought defeat to Satan.

6. To give us an example of a holy life – Christ was and is the only One who is perfect in His life and in his teachings. It was necessary that we have an illustration of what God wants us to be.

7. To prepare for the Second Advent – His first coming was necessary as a preparation for His second coming.

Now, let's look at Jesus Christ, God Incarnate. Jesus is revealed as the *Incarnate Word*, which *is the physical embodiment of who God is and a revelation of the nature and being of God.* In Christ are revealed the attributes that belong to God, especially His wisdom, power, holiness and love. Jesus Christ is *the Word* (John 1:1), the expression of what God is.

We know from the Scriptures that He was fully man. We know that the Incarnation of God was Christ becoming man. The word "incarnation" means "the act of assuming flesh," although, the actual word "incarnation" is not in the Bible.

The Old and New Testament Scriptures declare that Jesus was God in the flesh. In John 1:14, it states, "And the Word became flesh and dwelt among us, and we beheld His glory, the glory as of the only begotten of the Father, full of grace and truth." "*The Word* became flesh" indicates when Jesus was born as a baby in the manger at Bethlehem. *The Word*, who Jesus is, has always been. However, *the Word* became flesh, when He was born as a baby and lived on this earth.

He had always existed as the Son of God with the Father in heaven, but now He chose to come into the world in a human body. He dwelt among us. He was here for a short time. He lived on this earth for thirty-three years.

# CHAPTER 3

## *JESUS CHRIST: HIS LIFE ON EARTH*

When Jesus Christ came to earth as a human baby, but yet God, He came with a purpose and a mission. He came to save sinners! Christ came to earth as a human baby to fulfill God's plan of redemption for fallen man from the foundation of the world. In 1 Peter 1:20 we read, "He indeed was foreordained before the foundation of the world, but was manifest in these last times for you."

We read in Philippians 2:8-11, "And being found in appearance as a man, He humbled Himself and became obedient to death to the point of death, even the death of the cross. Therefore God also has highly exalted Him and given Him the name which is above every name, that at the name of Jesus every knee shall bow, of those in heaven, and of those on earth, and of those under the earth, and that every tongue should confess that Jesus Christ is Lord, to the glory of God the Father."

We, as sinners, needed a savior who could absolutely pay our sin debt in full. Otherwise, we would be *eternally* separated from God. Remember, God cannot look at sin. He is a holy and just God. If Jesus had never died, our punishment for sin would be death, separation from God. "For the wages of sin is death, but the gift of God is eternal life in Christ Jesus our Lord" (Romans 6: 23). The word "death" in this verse means *eternally separated from God.*

## *HIS BIRTH*

Let's talk about Jesus' virgin birth. His birth was different from any other birth. Mary was the mother of Jesus, humanly speaking. God chose her to be the woman through which He would send His Son into the world. The birth of Christ was a supernatural event. He was conceived by the Holy Spirit, yet He was human.

Mary was a young lady who theologians believe to have been around fourteen or fifteen years of age. The custom in those days was for women to marry young. Ladies, can you imagine marrying at this age? I cannot. I was too busy trying to pass my learner's license test to drive a car or studying for an algebra test – certainly not marriage.

Let's read the story of how Jesus came to earth in Luke 1:26-29. "Now in the sixth month the angel Gabriel was sent by God to a city of Galilee called Nazareth, to a virgin betrothed to a man whose name was Joseph, of the house of David. The virgin's name was Mary. And having come in, the angel said to her, 'Rejoice, highly favored one, the Lord is with you; blessed are you among women!' But when she saw him, she was troubled at his saying, and considered what manner of greeting this was."

The angel addressed Mary as one who was "highly favored," one to whom the Lord was visiting with special privilege. Two points should be noted here: (1) The angel *did not worship* Mary *or pray to her*; he simply greeted her. (2) He *did not* say that she was "full of grace," but highly favored.[49]

Also, in verse 29, we read, " . . . she was troubled at his saying, and considered what manner of greeting this was." This verse shows us that she was human just like us. Ladies, could you imagine being Mary at this point? I, no doubt, would have been troubled as well. An angel visits you and tells you this. Can you just imagine an angel appearing to you? What would you have done? I cannot imagine what she felt.

Let's continue with what the angel told Mary in Luke 1:30-38. "Then the angel said to her, 'Do not be afraid, Mary, for you have found favor with God. And behold, you will conceive in your womb and bring forth a Son, and shall call His name Jesus. He will be great, and will be called the Son of the Highest; and the Lord God will give Him the throne of his father David.'

'And He will reign over the house of Jacob forever, and of His kingdom there will be no end.' Then Mary said to the angel, 'How can this be, since I do not know a man?' And the angel answered and said to her, 'The Holy Spirit will come upon you, and the power of the Highest, will overshadow you; therefore, also, that Holy One who is to be born will be called the Son of God.' 'Now indeed, Elizabeth your relative has also conceived a son in her old age; and this is now the sixth month for her who was called barren. 'For with God nothing will be impossible.' Then Mary said, 'Behold the maidservant of the Lord! Let it be to me according to your word. And the angel departed from her.'"

Let's revisit Joseph's engagement to Mary. Marriages were arranged for individuals by parents, and contracts were negotiated. After this was accomplished, the individuals were considered married and were called husband and wife. They did not, however, begin to live together. Instead the woman continued to live with her parents and the man with his for one year.[50]

The waiting period was to demonstrate the faithfulness of the pledge of purity given concerning the bride. If she was found to be with child in this period, she obviously was not pure, but had been involved in an unfaithful sexual relationship. Therefore, the marriage was annulled.[51]

If, however, the one-year waiting period demonstrated the purity of the bride, the husband would then go to the house of the bride's parents and in a grand processional march lead his bride back to his home. There they would begin to live together as husband and wife and consummate their marriage physically.[52]

I remember my engagement and marriage. It was so exciting! When Rick proposed to me, I was so thrilled. The engagement and wedding were just wonderful! On our honeymoon night, we spent the night in a unique hotel in downtown Chattanooga, and when I opened the door to the hotel room, it was full of presents. It was like a fairy tale. Then we flew to Aruba. Most women will never forget their engagements and weddings. I know that I will always remember mine. Marriage, when handled the way that the Lord Jesus would have them to be, is wonderful.

While we are on the subject of marriage, let's read about what the Lord says in regards to marriages. In Hebrews 13:4 we read, "Marriage is honorable among all, and the bed undefiled; but fornicators and adulterers God will judge."

Now, let's return to Joseph and Mary. They were in their one-year waiting period when Mary was found to be with child. They had never had sexual intercourse and Mary herself had been faithful. Let's read Matthew 1:18-19. "Now the birth of Jesus Christ was as follows: After His mother Mary was betrothed to Joseph, before they came together, she was found with child of the Holy Spirit. Then Joseph her husband, being a just man, and not wanting to make her a public example, was minded to put her away secretly."

Let's think about these verses for a minute. How do you think Joseph felt about this? Mary is pregnant. His heart was probably broken. However, we can tell that he loved Mary by his actions. As we just read, " . . . Joseph her husband, being a just man, and not wanting to make her a public example, was minded to put her away secretly."

We know that Joseph loved her because he was minded to put her away secretly. But, let's look at what happens next!

I can hardly wait! In Matthew 1:20-21 we read, "But while he thought about these things, behold an angel of the Lord appeared to him in a dream, saying, 'Joseph, son of David, do not be afraid to take to you Mary your wife, for that which is conceived in her is of the Holy Spirit. And she will bring forth a Son, and you shall call His name Jesus, for He will save His people from their sins.'"

Have you ever experienced a situation like this when you had made up your mind about something only to find that right before you went through with it, the Lord God intervened? This is what happened to Joseph. All of a sudden, an angel of the Lord appears and explains it to Joseph. You know he was relieved. He knew then that it was God's plan.

Let's see what happens next. Let's read Matthew 1:24-25. "Then Joseph, being aroused from sleep, did as the angel of the Lord commanded him and took to him his wife, and did not know her till she had brought forth her firstborn Son. And he called His name Jesus."

Joseph violated all custom by immediately taking Mary into his home rather than waiting till the one-year time period of betrothal had passed. Joseph was probably thinking about what would be best for Mary in her condition. He brought her home and began to care and provide for her. But there was *no* sexual relationship between them *until* after the *birth* of the Child, Jesus. [53]

Have you noticed how Mary and Joseph were obedient to the Lord God? The angel appeared to Mary in Luke 1:38. "Then Mary said, 'Behold the *maidservant* of the Lord! Let it be to me according to your word.' And the angel departed from her." She acknowledged herself to be a maidservant of the Lord. The definition for a "maidservant" is "a woman servant." She was obedient to what God called her to do. She said, ". . . Let it be according to your word."

Women, are we like Mary? Are we obedient to the Lord? Or, are we afraid that God will call us to do something that we do not want to do? Mary was obedient. Those of us who have been born again need to be as well.

Was Joseph obedient? Let's read Matthew 1:24-25 again. "Then Joseph, being aroused from sleep, did as the angel of the Lord commanded him and took to him his wife, and did not know her till she had brought forth her firstborn Son. And he called His name Jesus." From these verses, we see that Joseph was obedient and did as he was commanded to do.

If you are a believer in Jesus Christ, you should be obedient to what He would have you to do. It may not be easy, but you and I need to obey God. Disobedience is a serious matter.

Let's see what happens next. Let's read Luke 2:1-5. "And it came to pass in those days that a decree went out from Caesar Augustus that all the world should be registered.

This census first took place while Quirinius was governing Syria. So all went to be registered, everyone to his own city. Joseph also went up from Galilee, out of the city of Nazareth, into Judaea, to the city of David, which is called Bethlehem, because he was of the house and lineage of David, to be registered with Mary, his betrothed wife, who was with child."

Mary accompanied Joseph for several reasons. The couple knew that she would have the Baby during the time Joseph was gone, and they most likely did not want to be separated at that event. Also, both of them knew that the Child was the Messiah. They would have known that the Messiah was to be born in Bethlehem (Micah 5:2). [54]

Bethlehem was a town six miles south of Jerusalem. Jesus was born towards the end of Herod the Great's reign as king of the Jews (37-4 B.C.).

Let's continue with the story. In Luke 2:6-7 we read, "So it was that, while they were there, the days were completed for her to be delivered. And she brought forth her firstborn

Son, and wrapped Him in swaddling cloths and laid Him in a manger; because there was no room for them in the inn." Notice that verse 7 states, ". . . her firstborn Son." Mary went on to have other children, giving Jesus four brothers.

We read this in Mark 6:3. "'Is this not the carpenter, the Son of Mary, and brother of James, Joses, Judas, and Simon? And are not His sisters here with us?' So they were offended at Him."

Let's consider the swaddling cloths in which Mary wrapped Jesus. The swaddling cloths were long narrow strips of cloth wrapped around a newborn infant to restrict movement.[55]

Jesus was laid in a manger. Have you ever wondered why God chose a manger for Jesus' bed? The dictionary defines a "manger" as "a trough for animal food." At the time of Jesus' birth, it was probably cold. The manger may have been cold, dark and dirty as well.

Let's continue with this story in Luke 2:8-12. "Now there were in the same country shepherds living out in the fields, keeping watch over their flock by night. And behold, an angel of the Lord stood before them, and the glory of the Lord shone around them, and they were greatly afraid. Then the angel said to them, 'Do not be afraid, for behold, I bring you good tidings of great joy, which will be to all people. For there is born to you this day in the city of David a Savior, who is Christ the Lord. And this will be the sign to you: you will find a Babe wrapped in swaddling cloths, lying in a manger."

Let's pause here for a moment. The first intimation of this unique birth was not given to the religious leaders in Jerusalem, but to contemplative shepherds on Judean hillsides, humble men who were faithful at their work.[56]

Let's revisit verse 12. "And this will be the sign to you: you will find a Babe wrapped in swaddling clothes, lying in a manger." It was the Lord telling them about finding the Babe. How else would they have known? The angel of the Lord told them precisely how they would find Jesus – wrapped in swaddling cloths and lying in a manger.

Before we go any further, let's distinguish between the divine and human natures of Jesus. Jesus Christ is both fully God and fully man (see Philippians 2:5-11). Humanly speaking, Mary was the mother of Jesus. However, she was not the mother of God. The expression "mother of God" is not found anywhere in the Bible. As God, He had no beginning and He was Mary's Creator. He created Mary just like He created us. Therefore, as God, He could not possibly have a mother. Mary cannot be the mother of God the Father or the mother of God the Holy Spirit. In the same way, she was *not* the mother of God the Son.[57]

For you see, God the Father, God the Son, and God the Holy Spirit are one. We read this in 1 John 5:7. "For there are three that bear witness in heaven: the Father, the Word, and the Holy Spirit; and these three are one."

God does not have a mother. In Genesis 1:1 it says, "In the beginning God created the heavens and the earth." God encompasses – God the Father, God the Son and God the Holy Spirit.

Mary is to be respected as the earthly mother of Jesus. She was human and the vessel that God chose to bring Jesus into this world. Scripture is extremely clear in stating that Mary was the true mother of Jesus Christ according to His human nature. However, He was already in existence but came to this earth in human form.

Mary is called the mother of Jesus, as stated in Acts 1:14. "These all continued with one accord in prayer and supplication, with the women and Mary the mother of Jesus, and with His brothers."

## HIS CHILDHOOD

Let's read about Jesus' childhood. Let's begin in Matthew 2:11. "And when they had come into the house, they saw the young Child with Mary His mother, and fell down and worshiped Him. And when they had opened their treasures, they presented gifts to Him: gold, frankincense and myrrh."

Let's continue in Luke 2:21-24. "And when eight days were completed for the circumcision of the Child, His name was called Jesus, the name given by the angel before He was conceived in the womb. Now when the days of her purification according to the Law of Moses were completed, they brought Him to Jerusalem, to present Him to the Lord; (as it is written in the law of the Lord, 'Every male who opens the womb shall be called holy to the Lord'), and to offer a sacrifice according to what is said in the law of the Lord, 'A pair of turtledoves or two young pigeons.'"

The couple was required by the law not only to have Jesus circumcised (Leviticus 12:3) but also to present their firstborn to God (Exodus 13:2, 12) thirty-three days later and to bring an offering for Mary's purification after childbirth (Leviticus 12:1-8).[58]

Let's read in Leviticus 12:1-4 about a woman's purification. "Then the Lord spoke to Moses, saying, 'Speak to the children of Israel, saying: If a woman has conceived, and borne a male child, then she shall be unclean seven days; as in the days of her customary impurity she shall be unclean. And on the eighth day the flesh of his foreskin shall be circumcised. She shall then continue in the blood of *her* purification thirty-three days. She shall not touch any hallowed thing, nor come into the sanctuary until the days of her purification are fulfilled.'"

The word "purification" means "the act of making oneself clean and pure before God and men." The Mosaic Law provided instructions for both physical and spiritual purification.[59]

So we read that Mary was unclean and had to go through the purification process, which means she was human. She was unclean, just as we are.

Let's continue looking at the early life of Jesus. He grew up in Nazareth, a town of Galilee. There He was raised by Mary and Joseph, a carpenter by trade. Hence, He was known as

"Jesus of Nazareth" or more fully "Jesus of Nazareth, the son of Joseph" (John 1:45). Jesus was Mary's firstborn child; He had four brothers – James, Joses, Judas, and Simon – and an unspecified number of sisters (Mark 6:3). Joseph apparently died before Jesus began His public ministry. Mary, with the rest of the family, lived on and became a member of the church of Jerusalem after Jesus' death and resurrection. [60]

Then we see in Luke 2:40, "And the Child grew and became strong in spirit, filled with wisdom; and the grace of God was upon Him." He grew in the normal growth of a child, which is set forth below:

1. *His physical growth* – and stature. He grew and became strong in spirit. He passed through the usual stages of physical development, learning to walk, talk, play and work. Because of this He can sympathize with us in every stage of our growth.[61]

2. *His mental growth* – increased in wisdom. He grew in wisdom, that is, in the practical application of this knowledge to the problems of life.[62]

3. *His spiritual growth* – The favor of God was upon Him. He walked in fellowship with God and in dependence of the Holy Spirit.[63]

4. *His social growth* – in favor with men.[64]

Let's continue to read Luke 2:41-45. "His parents went to Jerusalem every year at the Feast of the Passover. And when He was twelve years old, they went up to Jerusalem according to the custom of the feast. When they had finished the days, as they returned, the Boy Jesus lingered behind in Jerusalem. And Joseph and His mother did not know it; but supposing Him to have been in the company, they went a day's journey, and sought Him among their relatives and acquaintances. So when they did not find Him, they returned to Jerusalem, seeking Him."

Parents, can you relate? Have you ever lost your child? That would be a terrible experience.

When I think of a lost child, I remember a vacation that Rick and I took to Virginia Beach. We walked up and down the strip by the beach until we decided to take a break and sit on a bench. While we were sitting a little boy, who was around seven years of age, walked by calling "Mom! Mom!" I realized he was lost. So, I jumped up and went after him.

The strip at the beach was getting crowded. The Blue Angels, the U.S. Navy's Flight Demonstration Squadron, were supposed to fly over and a parachuting was to take place and people were gathering.

Rick followed me as I caught up with the little boy. At first, he wanted nothing to do with me. His mom taught him well to not talk to strangers! After a little coaxing, I convinced him that we would find his mom. Rick asked him if he remembered his hotel. He did.

We went to the hotel and the staff called the police. They came and talked to the little boy. Well, at this point, he and I had bonded. I wanted to make sure that he was with his parents before the night was over. The little boy had to stay with the policeman. However, he did tell us that his mom was wearing red. Rick and I returned to the strip and looked for a woman in red and called out the little boy's mom's name.

After walking up and down the strip in search of his mom, Rick saw him with his family and the police. We talked with his parents, who said that they had turned to look at a restaurant menu and apparently the little boy kept walking. They were so thankful to have found him. The mom, of course, was crying and, incidentally, she did not have on red. The Lord answered my prayer. Rick and I were relieved.

Let's return to Joseph and Mary. Can you just imagine what was going on in their minds while they were trying to find Jesus?

Let's see what happens next. Let's read Luke 2:46. "Now so it was that after three days they found Him in the temple, sitting in the midst of the teachers, both listening to them and asking them questions." The three days in this verse refer to the time since Mary and Joseph left Jerusalem to return home. You will recall that they left Jerusalem and traveled a day's journey. They returned to Jerusalem on the second day and found Jesus the next day.

Let's look again at where they found Him – in the temple, sitting in the midst of the teachers, both hearing them and asking them questions. He was twelve! And He was in the temple, sitting in the midst of the teachers. Let that sink into your mind! He was corresponding with the teachers of the Law, listening and asking questions. Were those who heard Him astonished? Yes. Let's read about this in Luke 2:47. "And all who heard Him were astounded at His understanding and answers." They were amazed!

In those days, a Jewish boy became a son of the law at the age of twelve. In today's society, a 12-year-old child is a seventh grader in school. What do 12-year-old children do in today's society? Many of them hang out with friends and go to movies. However, Jesus was in the temple sitting in the midst of the teachers.

Now let's read what happened when His parents found Him. "So when they saw Him, they were amazed; and His mother said to Him, 'Son, why have You done this to us?' Look, Your father and I have sought You anxiously" (Luke 2:48).

Let's stop here for a moment. This verse confirms that Mary was human. If she had been perfect or without sin, she would have known where Jesus was and what He was doing. But, she was anxiously searching for Him. She was an anxious mom, who was trying to find her son. Let me say that we should respect Mary as the mother of Jesus, humanly speaking. However, she was not God, nor was she on the same level as God. She trusted Jesus. We see how she trusted Jesus with the miracle of the water turned into wine. Let's read John 2:5. "His mother said to the servants, 'Whatever He says to you, do *it*.'"

Let's return to see how Jesus responded to his mother. "'And He said to them, 'Why did you seek Me? Did you not know that I must be about My Father's business?' But they did not understand the statement which He spoke to them" (Luke 2:49-50).

The Lord's answer, His first recorded words, shows that He was fully aware of His identity as the Son of God and of His divine mission as well. At the time, they did not understand what He meant by His cryptic remark. It was an unusual thing for a 12-year-old boy to say! [65]

## HIS ADULT MINISTRY

Let's read Luke 3:23 and see when Jesus began His ministry. "Now Jesus Himself began His ministry at about thirty years of age . . ." He opens His public ministry at about the age of thirty by being baptized in the Jordan River.[66]

Matthew, Mark, Luke, and John record this momentous occasion in the life of Jesus that signaled the beginning of His public ministry. Luke condensed the account more than the other Gospel writers. The purpose of Jesus' baptism was to anoint Him with the Spirit and to authenticate Him by the Father for beginning His ministry.

Each person of the Godhead was involved in the activity of the Son on earth, including His baptism. The *Son* was baptized, the *Holy Spirit* descended on Him, and the *Father* spoke approvingly of Him. In His baptism, Jesus identified Himself with sinners though He was not a sinner.[67] The baptism of Jesus is one of the three times when God spoke from heaven in connection with the ministry of His own dear Son. For thirty years, the eye of God had examined that flawless life in Nazareth; here God's verdict was, "I am well pleased."

Let's read about Jesus' baptism in Luke 3:21-22. "When all the people were baptized, it came to pass that Jesus also was baptized; and while He prayed, the heaven was opened. And the Holy Spirit descended in bodily form like a dove upon Him, and a voice came from heaven which said, 'You are My beloved Son; in You I am well pleased.'"

Think about it! While Jesus prayed, the heaven was opened. Can you just imagine the heaven opening? And the Holy Spirit descending in bodily form like a dove upon Him and a voice came from heaven which said, "You are My beloved Son; in You I am well pleased." How exciting! How pleased was God in His Son? Well pleased.

Scripture offers several reasons for the baptism of Christ: [68]

1. To "fulfill all righteousness" (Matthew 3:15). J.W. Shepherd says: "From earliest times, it has always been a question why Jesus went and was baptized. There have been many explanations, as to why He took His place among the penitents and submitted to the rite, which symbolized the cleansing away of sin. The true reason is in the reply of Jesus: 'Suffer it now; it is becoming for us to fulfill all (vicarious) righteousness.'" [69]

Jesus was born under the law, and in His infancy was circumcised and redeemed. At the age of twelve. He became a son of the law. He later paid the temple tax, though as the Son of God, He should have been exempted. It was fitting that He should fill out all the ordinances of the Abrahamic covenant to completion. From a later deliverance, we know that He came not to abrogate the Mosaic Law but to fill it out, giving it a deeper meaning (Matthew 5:17). Throughout His life He fulfilled the law that He might redeem them that were under the law (Galatians 4:4-5).[70]

2. A second reason for Christ's baptism is given in John 1:33-34: "I did not know Him, but He who sent me to baptize with water said to me, 'Upon whom you see the Spirit descending, and remaining on Him, this is He who baptizes with the Holy Spirit.' 'And I have seen and testified that this is the Son of God.'" John recognized Jesus as the Messiah when He presented Himself for baptism, but John was not permitted to reveal to Israel what he, by the Spirit, understood. It was only after the Spirit descended that John could make a public announcement that the One whom He had promised had now arrived and had begun His ministry. The baptism, then, was to release John to make a public announcement concerning the coming of Christ.[71]

3. The third reason for Christ's baptism was that He might identify Himself with the believing remnant in Israel.[72]

4. Lastly, Jesus was baptized to identify Himself with sinners. Sinners were coming to John to confess their sin, to confess their need of a Savior, and to give an outward sign of their faith that the Savior would come who would redeem them from sin. Jesus Christ came to identify Himself with sinners so that through that identification He might become their substitute.[73]

Let's discuss the issue of baptism. Who needs to be baptized? Those who have been born again. Let's read Colossians 2:12. "Buried with Him in baptism, in which you also were raised with *Him* through faith in the working of God, who raised Him from the dead." The teaching here is that we have not only died with Christ, but we have been buried with Him.

This was typified at our baptism. It took place at the time of our conversion, but we expressed it in public confession when we went into the waters of baptism.[74]

Let's see what happens after Jesus was baptized. We read in Matthew 4:1. "Then Jesus was led up by the Spirit into the wilderness to be tempted by the devil." It may be strange that Jesus should be led up by the Spirit into temptation. Why should the Holy Spirit lead Him into such an encounter? The answer is that this temptation was necessary to demonstrate His moral fitness to do the work for which He had come into the world. [75]

Let's return to Genesis for a moment. The first Adam proved how unfit he was when he met Satan in the garden of Eden. However, in these temptations, the last Adam, Jesus, hits Satan head-on and emerges unscathed. I listened to a message from Rev. E.V. Hill on these temptations of Jesus. He said that Jesus was giving us, as believers in Christ, an example to follow when we are tempted.

Let's see how Jesus responded to these temptations. We read in Matthew 4:3-4, "Now when the tempter came to Him, he said, 'If You are the Son of God, command that these stones become bread.' But He answered and said, *'It is written,* man shall not live by bread alone, but by every word that proceeds from the mouth of God.'"

We read of the second temptation in Matthew 4:5-7. "Then the devil took Him up into the holy city, set Him on the pinnacle of the temple, and said to Him, 'If you are the Son of God, throw Yourself down. For it is written: 'He shall give His angels charge over you,' and, 'in their hands they shall bear you up, lest you dash your foot against a stone.' Jesus said to him, 'It is written again, You shall not tempt the Lord your God.'"

The third temptation was in Matthew 4:8-10. "Again, the devil took Him up on an exceedingly high mountain, and showed Him all the kingdoms of the world and their glory.

And he said to Him, 'All these things I will give You if You will fall down and worship me.' Then Jesus said to him, 'Away with you, Satan! *For it is written,* you shall worship the Lord your God, and Him only you shall serve.'"

In all three of these temptations, how did Jesus respond to Satan? He responded to Satan by saying, "It is written or It is also written and quoting the Word." He quoted the Word to him because He is the Word. We read this in John 1:1. "In the beginning was The Word, and The Word was with God, and The Word was God." So, who is *The Word*? Jesus Christ. Furthermore, Jesus is called "The Word of God" in Revelation 19:13. "He was clothed with a robe dipped in blood, and *His name* is called *The Word of God.*"

When we are tempted by Satan, we should respond by saying, "It is written" and quote the verses of the Bible to him that deal with that temptation. This is one reason why it is so important that believers in Christ *know* the Bible.

For example, one area in my life where I struggle is fear. Sometimes, I am just overwhelmed with fear. I quote 2 Timothy 1:7. "For God has not given us a spirit of fear, but of power and of love and of a sound mind." I say this Scripture out loud and sometimes I repeat it several times. In rebuking the spirit of fear in the name of Jesus, the fear leaves me.

Fear is a very strong and unpleasant emotion. There are many different ways that fear can surface in our lives. Some of the ways are fear of illness, fear of death, fear of financial problems, fear of losing a spouse or child, or fear of losing your job. It is so important that we keep our focus on Jesus and not on ourselves or our situations. What does God tell us to do when we are afraid? The answer is in Psalm 56:3. "Whenever I am afraid, I will trust in You." Choose to trust Jesus Christ in every situation.

When we take our eyes off Jesus, we have fear, worry, depression, and other problems. Whether it is focusing on a marriage going the wrong way, dwelling on a stressful financial situation, worrying about a rebellious child or stressing over a job issue, we need to get on our knees and cry out to our Father. He can do something about it. He can do the impossible. We read in Luke 1:37, "For with God nothing will be impossible."

When I think of someone who had fear or was afraid, I think of Peter. We read this account of Peter in Matthew 14:24-32. "But the boat was now in the middle of the sea, tossed by the waves, for the wind was contrary. Now in the fourth watch of the night Jesus went to them, walking on the sea. And when the disciples saw Him walking on the sea, they were troubled, saying, 'It is a ghost!' and they cried out for fear. But immediately Jesus spoke to them, saying, 'Be of good cheer! It is I; do not be afraid.'

And Peter answered Him and said, 'Lord, if it is You, command me to come to You on the water.' So He said, 'Come.' And when Peter had come down out of the boat, he walked on the water to go to Jesus. But when he saw that the wind was boisterous, he was afraid; and beginning to sink he cried out, saying, 'Lord, save me!' And immediately Jesus stretched out *His* hand and caught him, and said to him, 'O you of little faith, why did you doubt?' And when they got into the boat, the wind ceased."

I love this story. I can relate, can you? Let's revisit it. In verse 25, the "fourth watch" means between 3:00 and 6:00 a.m. The disciples cried out because they thought Jesus was a ghost. Can you relate? I can. I would be crying out as well. How many times do we cry out when we are in despair, troubled, perplexed, upset – tossed in a storm of our own? Maybe we feel like Jesus is far away. However, if you are born again, He is right there with us. Our boat may be rocking back and forth, but the dangerous waves are under His feet.

Let's reread verses 26 and 27. "And when the disciples saw Him walking on the sea, they were troubled, saying, 'It is a ghost!' and they cried out for fear. But immediately Jesus spoke to them, saying, 'Be of good cheer! It is I; do not be afraid.'" Notice that when Jesus spoke, the disciples knew His voice. Do you know His voice when He speaks to you? Then we see that Peter wants to walk out to Him on the water. What does Jesus tell him? Come. Peter goes. He was walking on the water! Jesus made the impossible possible! Imagine – walking on water!

But while Peter is walking on the water, what happened? He saw the wind and was afraid. I can empathize with Peter. I am terrified of storms. Rick and I frequently visit Hilton Head in South Carolina. When it is hurricane season, I tell Rick that with the first sign of storms, we are out of there. However, Rick would love to ride out a hurricane, which must be a man thing. It certainly is not mine!

Let's return to Peter. As a result of his seeing that the wind was boisterous, what happened next? He began to sink. Friend, how many times do we "begin to sink" in the problems of life and cry out to Jesus to save us? I have many times. But when he saw the wind, he began to sink. We are so much like Peter. When our eyes are focused on Jesus, we do not sink. The moment we take our eyes off of Jesus we sink.

What was Peter's cry to Jesus? "Lord, save me!" I love this next part. "And immediately Jesus stretched out *His* hand and caught him, and said to him, 'O you of little faith, why did you doubt?'" (Matthew 14:31). I can just see Jesus stretching forth His hand to me, time and time again. There has been so many times in my life that He has saved me from disasters. However, I am most grateful that He has saved me from hell and has given me eternal life with Him. His love overwhelms me!

How many times have you witnessed Jesus performing the impossible in your life? Has He healed you when the doctors gave you no hope? Has He restored your marriage? Let's see what Jesus said in Matthew 19:26. "But Jesus looked at them and said to them, 'With men this is impossible, but with God all things are possible.'"

Let's continue with the adult ministry of Jesus. Jesus' time on the earth included choosing twelve disciples. Let's read about this in Matthew 10:1-4. "And when He had called His twelve disciples to Him, He gave them power over unclean spirits, to cast them out, and to heal all kinds of sickness and all kinds of disease. Now the names of the twelve apostles are these: first, Simon, who is called Peter, and Andrew his brother; James the son of Zebedee, and John his brother; Philip and Bartholomew; Thomas and Matthew the tax collector; James the son of Alphaeus and Lebbaeus, whose surname was Thaddaeus; Simon the Cananite, and Judas Iscariot, who also betrayed Him."

Jesus also spoke many parables while He was on the earth. A parable is a short, simple story designed to communicate a spiritual truth, religious principle, or moral lesson a figure of speech in which truth is illustrated by a comparison or example drawn from everyday experiences.[76]

Jesus' characteristic method of teaching was through parables. His two best known parables are the parable of the lost son (Luke 15:11-32) and the parable of the Good Samaritan (Luke 10:25-37). Both of these parables illustrate God's love for sinners and God's command that we show compassion to all people. Most of Jesus' parables have one central point.[77]

For example, the parable of the Good Samaritan tells us of a "hated" Samaritan who proved to be a neighbor to a wounded man. He showed the traveler the mercy and compassion denied to him by the priest and the Levite, representatives of the established religion. The *one central point* of this parable is that we should extend compassion to others even those who are not of our own nationality, race or religion (Luke 10:25-37).[78] Other parables of Jesus are listed below:

## THE PARABLES IN MATTHEW

1. The Wheat and the Tares (13:24-30).

2. The Treasure Hidden in a Field (13:44).

3. The Pearl of Great Price (13:45-46).

4. The Dragnet (13:47-50).

5. The Unmerciful Servant (18:21-35).

6. The Workers in the Vineyard (20:1-16).

7. The Two Sons (21:28-32).

8. The Wedding Feast (22:1-14).

9. The Budding Fig Tree (24:32).

10. The Wise and the Foolish Virgins (25:1-13).

## THE PARABLES IN MARK

1. The Seed Growing Silently (4:26-29).

2. The Watchful Doorkeeper (13:32-37).

## THE PARABLES IN LUKE

1. The Creditor Who Had Two Debtors (7:40-47).

2. The Good Samaritan (10:25:37).

3. The Friend Who Came at Midnight (11:5-8).

4. The Rich Fool (12:13-21).

5. The Fruitless Fig Tree (13:6-9).

6. The Large Banquet (14:15-24).

7. The Cost of Following Jesus (14:25-34).

8. The Lost Sheep (15:3).

9. The Lost Coin (15:8-10).

10. The Lost Son (15:11-32).

11. The Unjust Steward (16:1-13).

12. The Rich Man and Lazarus (16:19).

13. The Condescending Master (17:7-10).

14. The Persistent Widow (18:1-8).

15. The Pharisee and the Tax Collector (18:9-14).

16. The Talents (19:11-27).

## THE PARABLES IN MATTHEW AND LUKE

1. The Two Builders (Rock and Sand) (Matthew 7:24-27; Luke 6:47-49).

2. The Leaven (Matthew 13:33; Luke 13: 20-21).

3. The Lost Sheep (Matthew 18:10-14; Luke 15:1-7).

4. The Wicked Vinegrowers (Matthew 21:33; Luke 20:9).

5. The Talents (Matthew 25:14-30; Luke 19:11).

## THE PARABLES IN MATTHEW, MARK AND LUKE

1.  The Lamp and the Lampstand (Matthew 5:15-16; Mark 4:21; Luke 8:16).

2.  The New Cloth on Old Garments (Matthew 9:16; Mark 2:21; Luke 5:36).

3.  The New Wine in Old Wineskins (Matthew 9:17; Mark 2:22; Luke 5:37-39).

4.  The House Divided Against Itself (Matthew 12:25-29; Mark 3:23-27; Luke 11:17-22).

5.  The Sower and the Seed (Matthew 13:1-23; Mark 4:1-20; Luke 8:4-15).

6.  The Mustard Seed (Matthew 13:31-32; Mark 4:30-32; Luke 13:18-19).

7.  The Wicked Vinedressers (Matthew 21:33-41; Mark 12:1-12; Luke 20:9-18).

8.  The Fig Tree (Matthew 24:32-35; Mark 13:28-31; Luke 21:29-33).

## THE PARABLES IN JOHN

1.  The Bread of Life (John 6:32-58).

2.  The Shepherd and the Sheep (John 10:1-18).

3.  The Vine and the Branches (John 15:1-8).

Furthermore, while Jesus was on the earth, He performed miracles.

These are listed below:

1. The Water into Wine

2. The Many Healings

3. The Healing of a Leper

4. The Healing of a Roman Centurion's Servant

5. The Healing of Peter's Mother-in-law

6. The Calming of the Storm at Sea

7. The Healing of the Wild Man of Gadara

8. The Healing of a Lame Man

9. The Healing of a Woman with a Hemorrhage

10. The Raising of Jarius' Daughter

11. The Healing of Two Blind Men

12. The Healing of a Demon-possessed Man

13. The Healing of a Man with a Withered Hand

14. The Feeding of 5,000 People

15. The Walking on the Sea

16. The Healing of the Syrophenician's Daughter

17. The Feeding of 4,000 People

18. The Healing of an Epileptic Boy

19. The Healing of Two Blind Men at Jericho

20. The Healing of a Man with an Unclean Spirit

21. The Healing of a Deaf and Speechless Man

22. The Healing of a Blind Man at Bethesda

23. The Healing of Blind Bartimaeus

24. The Miraculous Catch of Fish

25. The Raising of a Widow's Son

26. The Healing of a Stooped Woman

27. The Healing of a Man with the Dropsy

28. The Healing of Ten Lepers

29. The Healing of Malchus' Ear

30. The Healing of a Royal Official's Son

31. The Healing of a Lame Man at Bethesda

32. The Healing of a Blind Man

33. The Raising of Lazarus

From among the large number of his followers, Jesus selected twelve men to remain in his company for training that would enable them to share his preaching and healing ministry. When Jesus judged the time to be ripe, He sent out His twelve disciples two by two to proclaim the kingdom of God throughout the Jewish districts of Galilee.[79]

## THE CRUCIFIXION OF JESUS CHRIST

Let's look at the events that transpired prior to Jesus' crucifixion:

(1) *Jesus' Arrest.* Let's read Matthew 26:47-50. "And while He was still speaking, behold, Judas, one of the twelve, with a great multitude with swords and clubs, came from the chief priests and elders of the people. Now His betrayer had given them a sign, saying, 'Whomever I kiss, He is the One; seize Him.' Immediately he went up to Jesus and said, 'Greetings, Rabbi!' and kissed Him. But Jesus said to him, 'Friend, why have you come?' Then they came and laid hands on Jesus and took Him."

In Matthew 26:14-16, we read that Judas Iscariot agreed to betray Christ for thirty silver coins, which was the redemption price paid for a slave (Exodus 21:32).

(2) *Jesus' Trials.* Jesus had six trials, which were three religious trials and three civil trials. These are charted below:

### Jesus' Six Trials

### Religious Trials

1. Before Annas (John 18:12-14)

2. Before Caiaphas (Matthew 26:57-68)

3. Before the Sanhedrin (Matthew 27:1-2)

Jesus was charged in these "ecclesiastical" trials with blasphemy, claiming to be the Son of God, the Messiah.

## Civil Trials

4.  Before Pilate (John 18:28-38)

5.  Before Herold (Luke 23:6-12)

6.  Before Pilate (John 18:39-19-6)

Let's talk about the religious trials, which were with Israel. They showed the degree to which the Jewish leaders hated Jesus because they carelessly disregarded many of their own laws. There were other illegalities as well such as the regular place for the meeting of the Sanhedrin was in the Temple, but they met in the house of the high priest Caiaphas; the legal hour of meeting for trials was not at night; undue haste; seeking or bribing witnesses; neglecting to warn the witnesses solemnly before they should give evidence; forcing the accused to testify against Himself; judicial use of the prisoner's confession and failure to release the prisoner when there was failure of agreement between witnesses.[80]

Let's talk about the civil trials, which were with Rome. Israel could decide that Jesus should die. However, Rome had to execute Him. The Jews could not execute one legally, for Rome retained that authority. In order to carry out the sentence, the Sanhedrin had to obtain the approval of the Roman authorities. Therefore, in order to get permission from Rome, the Jews "led Jesus from Caiaphas to the palace of the Roman governor" (John 18:28).

Jesus suffered physically prior to the crucifixion. Some of these physical sufferings are:

(1) In Matthew 26:67: "Then they spat in His face and beat Him; and others struck Him with the palms of their hands,"

(2) In Matthew 27:26: " . . . when he had scourged Jesus, he delivered Him to be crucified."

(3) In Matthew 27:30: " . . . Then they spat on Him, and took the reed and struck Him on the head."

(4) In Mark 14:65: "Then some began to spit on Him, and to blindfold Him, and to beat Him, and to say to Him, 'Prophesy!' And the officers struck Him with the palms of their hands."

(5) In Mark 15:17: "And they clothed Him with purple; and they twisted a crown of thorns, put it on His head . . ."

In Matthew 27:26, the term "scourged" means that someone used a large whip with bits of sharp metal embedded in it was brought down across the back, each lash opening up the flesh and releasing streams of blood.[81] In Isaiah 53:5 we read, "But He was wounded for our transgressions, He was bruised for our iniquities; the chastisement for our peace was upon Him, and by His stripes we are healed."

Think about this. *Jesus was beaten, scourged, whipped and struck all prior to His crucifixion.* Furthermore, He had a crown of thorns put on His head. Have you ever stuck your finger with a thorn? It is very painful. Can you imagine how Jesus felt? Furthermore, they struck Him on the head repeatedly with their staffs. The pain and suffering that He went through – for us. They mocked Him. *Remember, this was all prior to His crucifixion!*

In Matthew 27:32-35 we read, "Now as they came out, they found a man of Cyrene, Simon by name. Him they compelled to bear His cross. And when they had come to a place called Golgotha, that is to say, place of a Skull, they gave Him sour wine mingled with gall to drink. But when He had tasted it, He would not drink. Then they crucified Him, and divided His garments, casting lots, that it might be fulfilled which was spoken by the prophet: 'They divided My garments among them, and for My clothing they cast lots."

Let's stop here for a moment. Crucifixion was the Romans' most severe form of execution so it was reserved only for slaves and criminals. No Roman citizen could be crucified. Crucifixion involved attaching the victim with nails through the wrists or with leather thongs to a crossbeam attached to a vertical stake. Sometimes blocks or pins were put on the stake to give the victim some support as he hung suspended from the crossbeam. At times, the feet were also nailed to the vertical stake.[82]

As the victim hung dangling by the arms, the blood could no longer circulate to his vital organs. Only by supporting himself on the seat or pin could the victim gain relief. But gradually exhaustion set in, and death followed, although usually not for several days. If the victim had been severely beaten, he would not live this long. To hasten death, the executioners sometimes broke the victim's legs with a club. Then he could no longer support his body to keep blood circulating, and death quickly followed. The cross was the most disgraceful and one of the cruelest instruments of death ever invented.[83]

Let's continue with Matthew 27:45-46. "Now from the sixth hour until the ninth hour there was darkness over all the land. And about the ninth hour Jesus cried out with a loud voice, saying, 'Eli, Eli, lama sabachthani?' that is, 'My God, my God, why have you forsaken Me?'"

When Christ cried, "Why have you forsaken Me?" He testified to the fact that He had, at this point, entered into spiritual death. He was separated from God as the sinner's Substitute. His physical death would soon follow as He fully tasted death for every man (see Hebrews 2:9).

Because God is Holy, He cannot overlook sin. On the contrary, He must punish it. The Lord Jesus had no sin of His own, but He took the guilt of our sins upon Himself. When

God, as Judge, looked down and saw our sins upon the sinless Substitute, He withdrew from the Son of His love.[84]

Now, let's read John 19:30. "So when Jesus had received the sour wine, He said, '*It is finished*!' And bowing His head, He gave up His spirit." At this point, *He had completed the mission that He came to earth to accomplish.* Jesus Christ laid down His life for us. He paid our sin debt that we could not pay. He paid it once and for all. "For God so loved the world that He gave His only begotten Son, *that whoever believes in Him should not perish but have everlasting life*" (John 3:16).

Let's see what happened in Matthew 27:51-52. "Then, behold, the veil of the temple was torn in two from top to bottom; and the earth quaked, and the rocks split, and the graves were opened; and many bodies of the saints who had fallen asleep were raised;"

Do you realize what verse 51 means? "Then, behold, the veil of the temple was torn in two from top to bottom . . ." It was torn by God from top to bottom, not bottom to top which would indicate man tore it.

When Jesus died, the heavy woven veil separating the two main rooms of the temple was torn by an Unseen Hand from top to bottom. Before the death of Christ, the veil had kept everyone, except for the high priest, from the Holiest Place where God dwelt. *Only one man* could enter the inner sanctuary, and he could only enter on one day of the year, the "Day of Atonement."

In Hebrews 10:20, we learn that the veil represented the body of Christ. Its rending pictured the giving of His body in death. Through His death, we have boldness to enter the Holiest by His blood. "Therefore, brethren, having boldness to enter the Holiest by the blood of Jesus, by a new and living way which He consecrated for us, through the veil, that is, His flesh" (Hebrews 10:19-20).

If you have been born again, you can enter God's presence boldly because of the blood sacrifice that Christ made for us. But let us never forget that the privilege was purchased for us at tremendous cost – the blood of Jesus.[85]

John Piper gives ten reasons why Jesus came to die from the Bible. They are:

(1)    *To give eternal life to all who believe on Him (Jesus Christ).* "And this is eternal life, that they may know You, the only true God, and Jesus Christ whom You have sent" (John 17:3).

(2)    *To bring us to God.* "For Christ also suffered once for sins, the just for the unjust, that He might bring us to God, being put to death in the flesh but made alive by the Spirit" (1 Peter 3:18).

(3)    *To take away our condemnation (to declare a person guilty and worthy of punishment – it is a judicial term)*[86]. "There is therefore now no condemnation to those who are in Christ Jesus, who do not walk according to the flesh, but according to the Spirit" (Romans 8:1).

(4)    *To show Jesus' own love for us.* "Just as the Son of Man did not come to be served, but to serve, and to give His life a ransom for many" (Matthew 20:28).

(5)    *To show God's love for sinners.* "For God so loved the world that He gave His only begotten Son, that whoever believes in Him should not perish but have everlasting life" (John 3:16).

(6)    *To reconcile us to God.* "For if when we were enemies we were reconciled to God through the death of His Son, much more, having been reconciled, we shall be saved by His life" (Romans 5:10).

(7) *So that we would escape the curse of the law.* "Christ has redeemed us from the curse of the law, having become a curse for us (for it is written, 'Cursed is everyone who hangs on a tree')" (Galatians 3:13).

(8) *To absorb the wrath of God.* "For the wages of sin is death, but the gift of God is eternal life in Christ Jesus our Lord" (Romans 6:23).

(9) *To give marriage its deepest meaning.* "Husbands, love your wives, just as Christ also loved the church and gave Himself for her" (Ephesians 5:25).

(10) *To destroy hostility between races.* "For He Himself is our peace, who has made both one, and has broken down the middle wall of separation, having abolished in His flesh the enmity, that is, the law of commandments contained in ordinances, so as to create in Himself one new man from the two, thus making peace, and that He might reconcile them both to God in one body through the cross, thereby putting to death the enmity" (Ephesians 2:14-16).

## THE BURIAL OF JESUS CHRIST

Let's read Matthew 27:57-60. "Now when evening had come, there came a rich man from Arimathea, named Joseph, who himself had also become a disciple of Jesus.

This man went to Pilate and asked for the body of Jesus. Then Pilate commanded the body to be given to him. When Joseph had taken the body, he wrapped it in a clean linen cloth, and laid it in his new tomb which he had hewn out of the rock; and he rolled a large stone against the door of the tomb, and departed." This tells us what took place at Jesus' burial.

## THE RESURRECTION OF JESUS CHRIST

Let's see what takes place at His resurrection! Let's read John 20:1-7. "Now on the first day of the week Mary Magdalene went to the tomb early, while it was still dark, and saw that the stone had been taken away from the tomb. Then she ran and came to Simon Peter, and to the other disciple, whom Jesus loved, and said to them, 'They have taken away the Lord out of the tomb, and we do not know where they have laid Him.'

"Peter therefore went out, and the other disciple, and were going to the tomb. So they both ran together, and the other disciple outran Peter and came to the tomb first. And he, stooping down and looking in, saw the linen cloths lying there; yet he did not go in. Then Simon Peter came, following him, and went into the tomb; and he saw the linen cloths lying there, and the handkerchief that had been around His head, not lying with the linen cloths, but folded together in a place by itself."

The fact that the strips of linen cloth were undistributed and that the burial cloth that had been around Jesus' head was neatly folded up by itself was evidence that the body had not been stolen. Furthermore, the condition of the cloths indicates that there was no undue haste associated with the Resurrection. Had there been, the cloths would not have been laid aside so neatly.[87]

In regards to His resurrection, let's recall what Jesus said in John 2:19-22. "Jesus answered and said to them, 'Destroy this temple, and in three days I will raise it up.' Then the Jews said, 'It has taken forty-six years to build this temple, and will You raise it up in three days?' But He was speaking of the temple of His body. Therefore, when He had risen from the dead, His disciples remembered that He had said this to them, and they believed the Scripture and the word which Jesus had said."

Let's look at the words in verse 19 again ". . . Destroy this temple, and in three days I will raise it up . . .." Only God could say that. Jesus' body is represented as the temple. He did rise again on the third day.

The resurrection of Christ is of paramount importance for several reasons:

(1) *It is the fundamental doctrine of Christianity.* Many admit the necessity of the death of Christ who deny the importance of the bodily resurrection of Christ. But that Christ's physical resurrection is vitally important is evident from the fundamental connection of this doctrine with Christianity. In 1 Corinthians 15:12-19, Paul shows that everything stands or falls with Christ's bodily resurrection. If Christ had not risen, preaching is vain (verse 14), the Corinthians' faith was vain (verse 14), and the apostles were false witnesses (verse 15), the Corinthians were yet in their sins (verse 17), those fallen asleep in Jesus have perished (verse 18) and Christians are of all men most to be pitied (verse 19). The resurrection is clearly an essential part of the Gospel.[88]

(2) *It has an important part in the application of salvation.* God raised Him up to his own right hand that He might be the head over all things to the church (Ephesians 1:20-22). His death, resurrection and ascension are preparatory to His bestowing gifts on men (Ephesians 4:7-13). And He must rise to be a Prince and Savior, to give repentance and remission of sins to Israel (Acts 5:31). The resurrection is essential to the application of the salvation provided by the death of Christ.[89]

(3) *It is important as an exhibition of divine power.* The standard of divine power often expressed in the Old Testament was the power with which the Lord brought Israel out of the land of Egypt. The annual Passover was a reminder of God's mighty hand (Exodus 12). In the New Testament, the standard power

is the power of God exhibited in the resurrection of Christ. It was impossible for Christ to be held in death's power (Acts 2:24). This same power that raised Christ from the dead is available to Christians.[90]

Let's see the results of Christ's resurrection.

(1) *It attests to Christ's deity.* Paul teaches that Christ "was declared with power to be the Son of God by the resurrection from the dead" (Romans 1:4). Christ had pointed forward to His resurrection as a sign that would be given the people of Israel (Matthew 12:38-40) and Paul declares that it was a sign of His deity.[91]

(2) *It assures the acceptance of Christ's work.* Paul writes that Christ "was delivered up because of our transgressions, and was raised because of our justification" (Romans 4:25). We can have the confidence that God has accepted Christ's sacrifice because He was raised from the dead.[92]

(3) *It has made Christ our high priest.* Through His resurrection from the dead, He became the *intercessor, executive,* and *protector* of His people (Romans 5:9). He not only delivers from bondage, but He also intercedes for His people in times of need.[93]

(4) *It provided for many additional blessings.* By Christ's resurrection, provision has been made for the personal realization of the salvation which He has provided in His bestowal of repentance, forgiveness, regeneration and the Holy Spirit (John 16:7, Acts 2:33, 3:26, 5:31, 1 Peter 1:3). Again, His resurrection is made the basis of assurance to the believer that all necessary power for life and service is available to him (Ephesians 1:18-20). If God could raise Christ from the dead, He is able to supply all the needs of the believer (Philippians

3:10). The resurrection of Christ is a guarantee that our bodies too will be raised from the dead (John 5:28). And again, the resurrection of Christ is God's concrete proof that there will be a judgment of the godly and the ungodly (Acts 10:42).[94]

Let's return to the resurrection of Jesus. Let's read John 20:10-16. "Then the disciples went away again to their own homes. But Mary stood outside by the tomb weeping, and as she wept she stooped down and looked into the tomb. And she saw two angels in white sitting, one at the head and the other at the feet, where the body of Jesus had lain. Then they said to her, 'Woman, why are you weeping?' She said to them, 'Because they have taken away my Lord, and I do not know where they have laid Him.'

Now when she had said this, she turned around and saw Jesus standing there, and did not know that it was Jesus. Jesus said to her, 'Woman, why are you weeping? Whom are you seeking?' She, supposing Him to be the gardener, said to Him, 'Sir, if you have carried Him away, tell me where You have laid Him, and I will take Him away.' Jesus said to her, 'Mary!' She turned and said to Him, 'Rabboni!' (which is to say, Teacher)."

Here you have a woman who loves her Lord and is upset because she can't find Him. She is crying. Then He said her name, "Mary." When I read this, I think about how personal Jesus Christ is. He knows my name! As we read earlier, Jesus is the Good Shepherd (see John 10:3), He calls His sheep by name and "they know His voice." She recognized His voice! She knew it was Jesus.

After Jesus' resurrection, He appeared twelve times. These appearances include:

(1)   The appearance to Mary Magdalene (see Mark 16:9).

(2)   The appearance to the other women on the way (see Matthew 28:9).

(3)   The appearance of Christ to the two on the road to Emmaus (see Mark 16:12).

(4)   The appearance of Christ to Simon Peter (see Luke 24:34).

(5)   The appearance of Christ to the ten apostles (see John 20:19-24).

(6)   The appearance to the eleven disciples (see John 20:26-20).

(7)   The appearance to the apostles at the Sea of Tiberias (see John 21:1-14).

(8)   The appearance to the apostles on the mount in Galilee (see Matthew 28:16-20).

(9)   The appearance to more than five hundred brethren at the same time (see 1 Corinthians 15:6).

(10)  The appearance to James (see 1 Corinthians 15:7).

(11)  The appearance to His disciples on the mount of the ascension (see Mark 16:19).

(12)  The appearance to Paul (see 1 Corinthians 15:8).

Jesus Christ was on the earth forty days after His resurrection. We read this in Acts 1:3. "To whom He also presented Himself alive after His suffering by many infallible proofs, being seen by them during forty days and speaking of the things pertaining to the kingdom of God."

## CHAPTER 4

## *JESUS CHRIST: HIS ASCENSION TO HEAVEN*

The New Testament teaches that Jesus Christ ascended to heaven after His resurrection. The Ascension of Christ – the breathtaking departure of the risen Christ from His earthly, bodily ministry among His followers to heaven. Since His birth in Bethlehem, which was by the miracle of the Incarnation – which means He was God in the flesh – Christ had lived physically on the earth. After His resurrection, He was on the earth for forty days. His earthly ministry ended with His ascension into heaven.

The ascension of Christ refers to His returning to heaven in His resurrected body. In Luke 24:50-53 we read of this account: "And He led them out as far as Bethany, and He lifted up His hands and blessed them. Now it came to pass, while He blessed them, that He was parted from them and carried up into heaven. And they worshiped Him, and returned to Jerusalem with great joy, and were continually in the temple praising and blessing God. Amen."

To a large extent the ascension was for the benefit of Jesus' followers. They could no longer expect His physical presence. They must now wait for the promised Holy Spirit through whom the work of Jesus would continue.[95]

The ascension marked the starting of Christ's intercession for believers in Him at the right hand of God. We read in Romans 8:34, "Who is he who condemns? It is Christ who died, and furthermore is also risen, who is even at the right hand of God, who also makes intercession for us."

If the Lord Jesus to whom all judgment has been committed does not pass sentence on the defendant but rather prays for him, then there is no one else who could have a valid reason for condemning him.[96]

Let's read Hebrews 7:25. "Therefore He is also able to save to the uttermost those who come to God through Him, since He always lives to make intercession for them." I love that verse! How is He able to save those who come to God through Him? He is able to save them *completely*. What does He live to do for those whom He saves? He lives *to intercede* for them. What a Savior! As believers in Christ, we have God's Son interceding for us to God the Father.

He is also able to save them for all time because His present ministry for them at God's right hand can never be interrupted by death.[97]

In His present position at the right hand of the Father, Christ fulfills the seven figures relating Him to the church. These figures are:

(1) Christ as the last Adam and head of the new creation.

(2) Christ as the head of the body of Christ.

(3) Christ as the great shepherd of His sheep.

(4) Christ as the true vine in relation to the branches.

(5) Christ as the chief cornerstone in relation to the church as stones of the building.

(6) Christ as our high priest in relationship to the church as a royal priesthood.

(7) Christ as the bridegroom in relation to the church as the bride. All of these figures are full of meaning in describing His present work. His chief ministry, however, is as our high priest representing the church before the throne of God.[98]

There are four important truths that are revealed in His work as high priest:[99]

(1) *As high priest over the true tabernacle on high, the Lord Jesus Christ has entered into heaven itself there to minister as Priest in behalf of those who are His own in the world (Hebrews 8:1-2).* The fact that He, when ascending, was received by His Father in heaven is evidence that His earthly ministry was accepted. That He sat down indicated that His work for the world was completed.[100]

(2) *As our high priest, Christ is the bestower of spiritual gifts.* According to the New Testament, a gift is a divine enablement wrought in and through the believer by the Spirit who indwells him. It is the Spirit working to accomplish certain divine purposes and using the one whom He indwells to that end. It is in no sense a human undertaking aided by the Spirit.[101]

(3) *The ascended Christ as priest ever lives to make intercession for His own.* This ministry began before He left the earth (John 17:1-26), is for the saved rather than for the unsaved (John 17:9), and will be continued in heaven as long as His own are in the world. His work of intercession has to do with the weakness, the helplessness, and the immaturity of the saints who are on the earth – things concerning which they are in no way guilty. The priestly intercession of Christ in not only effectual, but unending. The priests of old failed because of death; but Christ, because He ever lives, has an unchanging priesthood.[102]

(4) *Christ now appears for His own in the presence of God.* The child of God is often guilty of actual sin which would separate his fellowship with God were it not for his Advocate and what He wrought at His death. The effect of the Christian's sin upon himself is that he loses his fellowship with God, his joy, his peace and his power. On the other hand, these experiences are restored in infinite grace on the sole ground that he confess his sin (1 John 1:9) but it is more important to consider the Christian's sin in relation to the holy character of God.

Through the present priestly advocacy of Christ in heaven there is absolute safety and security for the Father's child even while he is sinning. An advocate is one who espouses and pleads the cause of another in the open courts. As advocate, Christ is now appearing in heaven for His own (Hebrews 9:24) when they sin (1 John 2:1). His pleading is said to be with the Father, and Satan is there also, ceasing not to accuse the brethren night and day before God (Revelation 12:10).[103]

Let me say that a child of God can lose fellowship with God because of unconfessed sin, but never sonship.

Jesus is also making preparations for those of us who have trusted in Him for our eternal future. "Let not your heart be troubled; you believe in God, believe also in Me. In My Father's house are many mansions; if it were not so, I would have told you. I go to prepare a place for you. And if I go and prepare a place for you, I will come again and receive you to Myself; that where I am, there you may be also. And where I go you know, and the way you know" (John 14:1-4).

Let's reread some of verse 4. " . . . And where I go you know, and the way you know." Let's continue with John 14: 5-7. "Thomas said to Him, 'Lord, we do not know where You are going, and how can we know the way?' Jesus said to him, *'I am the way, the truth, and the life. No one comes to the Father except through Me.* If you had known Me, you would have known My Father also; and from now on you know Him

131

and have seen Him." This is crystal clear. If you want to go to heaven, you *have* to go through Jesus. *He is the only Door!* Furthermore, in order to go to God, you *have* to go through His Son, Jesus. *There is no other way!*

Also, presently, Jesus continues to function as Lord of the church (see Revelation 1:10-20). He is also actively involved in the lives of His saints – people who are saved – and in the growth and development of His church (see Acts 1:4-5; 2:47).

Furthermore, Jesus is preparing His bride, the church. The New Testament pictures the spiritual relationship between Christ and His church as that of a husband and wife. The apostle Paul said, "Husbands, love your wives, just as Christ also loved the church and gave Himself for her, that He might sanctify and cleanse her with the washing of water by the word, that He might present her to Himself a glorious church, not having spot or wrinkle or such thing, but that she should be holy and without blemish." (Ephesians 5:25-27). Then we read in Revelation 19:7-9 about the Marriage of the Lamb in heaven. Christ is depicted as the Bridegroom whose wife – the church – has made herself ready for the wedding as the bride of Christ.[104] When speaking of "the church," it refers to the body of believers in Christ.

# CHAPTER 5

## *JESUS CHRIST: HIS ROLE IN THE FUTURE*

As we examined in Chapter 4, Christ is presently seated at the right hand of God the Father. We read this in Ephesians 1:20-21. "Which He worked in Christ when He raised Him from the dead and seated Him at His right hand in the heavenly places, far above all principality and power and might and dominion, and every name that is named, not only in this age but also in that which is to come." How awesome is that? Christ is seated at God's right hand, even as I write this. Not only that, He is interceding for believers in Him.

The next event to happen is the *Rapture*. Now, the term "Rapture" is not in the Bible. However, it is the event described in 1 Thessalonians 4:15-17. "For this we say to you by the word of the Lord, that we who are alive and remain until the coming of the Lord will by no means precede those who are asleep. For the Lord Himself will descend from heaven with a shout, with the voice of an archangel, and with the trumpet of God. And the dead in Christ will rise first. Then we who are alive and remain shall be caught up together with them in the clouds to meet the Lord in the air. And thus we shall always be with the Lord."

I do not know about you, but sometimes I just look up to the clouds and think one day Jesus will appear and call us, believers in Him, home. It does not matter where I am when He calls. I will be gone! If you think that the "Rockin' Roller

Coaster" at Disney World is fast, if you are a believer in Christ, this will happen in a flash! It will be one more of a ride!

Let's read 1 Corinthians 15:51-52. "Behold, I tell you a mystery: We shall not all sleep, but we shall all be changed – in a moment, in the twinkling of an eye, at the last trumpet. For the trumpet will sound, and the dead will be raised incorruptible, and we shall be changed." It is a mystery. A mystery is a truth previously unknown, but now revealed by God to the apostles and made known through them to us.[105]

Let's reread some of verse 51. "Behold, I tell you a mystery: We shall not all sleep, but we shall all be changed . . ." Not all believers will experience death. Some will be alive when the Lord Jesus returns. But whether you are asleep or still alive, you will be changed.

Think about it: " . . . in a moment, in the twinkling of an eye . . ." That is fast! It will happen that quickly! Let's re-read 1 Thessalonians 4:17. "Then we who are alive and remain shall be caught up together with them in the clouds to meet the Lord in the air. And thus we shall always be with the Lord." We, as believers in Christ, will meet our Lord in the air and will be with Him forever! Forever! Let that sink in! Not just for a day, a week or a month – *forever*!

The English word "Rapture" comes from the Latin word "raptus," which in Latin Bibles translates the Greek word "harpazo," used fourteen times in the New Testament. The basic meaning of the word is "to suddenly remove or snatch away." It is used by the New Testament writers in reference to stealing or plundering (Matthew 11:12, 12:29, 13:19, John 10:12-28-29) and removing (John 6:15, Acts 8:39, 23:10, Jude 23).[106]

In this manner, the entire church will be removed from the scene of earth and will fulfill the promise of John 14 of being with Christ in the Father's house in heaven.[107]

After the Rapture, the earth will remain unchanged. People will continue with their lives. For example, if a person is at the grocery store and the Rapture takes place and they have never trusted Jesus Christ as their Lord and Savior, they will still be at the grocery store.

While we are talking about the Rapture, let me clarify that some people may think that it and the Second Coming of Jesus Christ are the same event. However, these are two totally different events. In the Rapture, Jesus Christ does not come to the earth. Rather, the saints, or those of us who have trusted Him as our Lord and Savior, will meet Him in the air. Furthermore, the Rapture takes place before the Tribulation.

*The Second Coming,* or it is described as a glorious appearing (Greek, epiphaino) *or epiphany,* is when Jesus Christ will return to this earth to judge the world and establish His messianic kingdom. It is one of the most significant events predicted in the entire Bible. Many of the psalms and all of the prophets refer to it, as do the apostles and our Lord Himself on numerous occasions. It will accomplish the completion of the first resurrection of the dead. It will initiate the final phase of Christ's victory over Satan. Most importantly, it will vindicate His absolute trustworthiness because He promised so many times that He would return in the glory of His Father.[108] Furthermore, it takes place *after* the Tribulation.

You may wonder what happens to everyone else left on the earth? Good question. It will not be good for them. Those who remain on the earth will begin a time called the *"Tribulation"* period. The church or those who have been saved is now gone. What happens next for the believers? The Judgment Seat of Christ takes place. In Jeremiah 32:19 we read, "You are great in counsel and mighty in work, for Your eyes are open to all the ways of the sons of men, to give everyone according to his ways and according to the fruit of his doings."

Every person of the human race is accountable to God. God will judge the believer and the unbeliever. The Great White Throne Judgment (see Revelation 20:15) will judge the unbelievers. The Judgment Seat of Christ (see 2 Corinthians 5:10) will judge the believers. At the Judgment Seat of Christ,

Christ will be the Judge ("And has given Him authority to execute judgment also, because He is the Son of Man" John 5:27).

Let me be clear that the Judgment Seat of Christ *will not be* to determine our status of salvation, but rather to determine our works. Let's read 2 Corinthians 5:10 in regards to the Judgment Seat of Christ. "For we must all appear before the Judgment Seat of Christ, that each one may receive the things done in the body, according to what he has done, whether good or bad."

Any person who has trusted in Jesus Christ for his or her salvation will never be condemned (express hate for, disapprove, sentence to death)[109] for their sins. We read in Romans 8:1, "There is therefore now no condemnation to those who are in Christ Jesus, who do not walk according to the flesh, but according to the Spirit." They are justified, declared righteous, and therefore stand in His grace (Romans 5:2) and not under His wrath (1:18) and possess eternal life (5:17-18, 21).[110]

This judgment is not optional. Everyone who has been born again must appear for judgment! What will be judged? The purpose of the judgment of believers at the Judgment Seat of Christ is to determine the worthiness or worthlessness of their works. The evaluation of the believer's works will include the works themselves, the quality with which they have been done, and the motivation of the heart.[111]

What a believer in Jesus Christ does for God really matters! In 1 Corinthians 3:12-13 we read, "Now if anyone builds on this foundation with gold, silver, precious stones, wood, hay, straw, each one's work will become clear; for the Day will declare it, because it will be revealed by fire; and the fire will test each one's work, of what sort it is."

The works will be of two kinds: good works and bad works. As defined by God, good works are designated by gold, silver and precious stones. They are produced in a believer who is walking in fellowship with God and who is controlled by the Holy Spirit. Good works are also called "the fruit of righteousness which comes through Jesus Christ, to the glory and praise of God" (Philippians 1:11). The power to produce good works comes directly from God, not from within man (see Philippians 2:13).[112]

Let's look at the bad works. Bad deeds *(phaulos)* are worthless in the sight of God. These could be called dead works or works of the flesh. The danger of producing works of the flesh is that the believer's labor is in vain (1 Corinthians 15:58), empty (1 Timothy 6:20, 2 Timothy 2:16), and worthless (Galatians 4:9, Titus 3:9, James 1:26). These are deeds produced in the energy of the flesh, apart from the power of the Spirit. Bad works also spring from wrong motives.[113]

The motivation for our works will also be revealed at the Judgment Seat of Christ. Jesus said, "For there is nothing covered that will not be revealed, nor hidden that will not be known. Therefore whatever you have spoken in the dark will be heard in the light, and what you have spoken in the ear in inner rooms will be proclaimed on the housetops" (Luke 12:2-3). Purposes give birth to behavior. The purpose or motivation of the heart validates or invalidates the actions of one's life.[114]

Believers will gain or lose rewards at the Judgment Seat of Christ. Works enduring through the fire of God's judgment will be rewarded (1 Corinthians 3:14). Works that do not survive the fire of judgment will lose their value. [115]

The giving out of the rewards will take place at this time as well. These rewards are to bring praise and glory to Christ because He empowered the believer to complete the task that He had for them to accomplish. The rewards are not to boast the ego of the believer.

There are also five crowns that are used as motivation for godly behavior:

(1) *The Incorruptible Crown.* "And everyone who competes for the prize is temperate in all things. Now they do it to obtain a perishable crown, but we for an imperishable crown" (1 Corinthians 9:25). As believers in Christ, we are in a race, and because we are in a race, we receive an incorruptible crown. In 2 Timothy 4:7 we read, "I have fought the good fight, I have finished the race, I have kept the faith."

(2) *The Crown of Rejoicing.* This is the soul winner's crown. Paul wrote to the Thessalonians, "For what is our hope, or joy, or crown of rejoicing? Is it not even you in the presence of our Lord Jesus Christ at His coming?" (1 Thessalonians 2:19). The evangelism of the lost people is a profound desire of God. He promises to reward those who will seek the lost on His behalf.

(3) *The Crown of Righteousness.* This crown is for those who wait for His appearing. Let's read 2 Timothy 4:8. "Finally there is laid up for me the crown of righteousness, which the Lord, the righteous Judge, will give to me on that Day, and not to me only but also to all who have loved His appearing." Are you waiting for His appearing?

(4) *The Crown of Life.* In regards to this crown, let's read Revelation 2:10. "Do not fear any of those things which you are about to suffer. Indeed, the devil is about to throw some of you into prison, that you may be tested, and you will have tribulation ten days. Be faithful until death, and I will give you the crown of life."

(5) *The Crown of Glory.* "And when the Chief Shepherd appears, you will receive the crown of glory that does not fade away" (1 Peter 5:4).

Now, let's return to the people on the earth. While the Judgment Seat of Christ is taking place for those who are saved, the people on the earth are going through the Tribulation period. This is called the Tribulation period because it is the seven-year period following the Rapture of the church (those who are saved) that will complete God's program in this present Age. The beginning of the Tribulation period is the onset of a series of events which will rapidly move on to a great culmination at the Second Coming of Christ. With the removal of the believers in Christ, the evil in the world will be in a way never before possible.

The Bible has a lot to say about these seven years, more than any other prophetic time period. The last three and a half years of this seven-year period is referred to as the *Great Tribulation* period. The Great Tribulation is mentioned in Revelation 7:14. "And I said to him, 'Sir, you know.' So he said to me, 'These are the ones who come out of the Great Tribulation, and washed their robes and made them white in the blood of the Lamb.'"

Let's talk about the Tribulation period. According to Daniel 9:27, when the dictator of the Middle East emerges as the "Prince that shall come" (Daniel 9:26), he will make a covenant with Israel for a seven-year period.[116] As a yet-future ruler, he will be the final head of the fourth empire, which is the Roman Empire.[117] This ruler is the Antichrist or the Beast.

Who is the *Antichrist*? The *Antichrist* or the *Beast* is an evil being who will set himself up against Christ and the people of God in the last days before the Second Coming of Christ. His primary work is deception, which also characterizes Satan in his attempts to undermine the work of God in the world.[118]

The Antichrist is also called the lawless one. "The coming of the lawless one is according to the working of Satan, with all power, signs, and lying wonders, and with all unrighteous deception among those who perish, because they did not receive the love of the truth, and they might be saved" (2 Thessalonians 2: 9-10). He will be empowered by Satan and will lead the final rebellion against God.

"Let no one deceive you by any means; for that Day will not come unless the falling away comes first, and the man of sin is revealed, the son of perdition, who opposes and exalts himself above all that is called God or that is worshiped, so that he sits as God in the temple of God, showing himself that he is God" (2 Thessalonians 2: 3-4). The term "lawlessness" is defined as sin. He is the man of sin, the very embodiment of sin and rebellion.

For you see, Satan tries to counterfeit everything that God does. For example, the Holy Trinity: God the Father, God the Son, and God the Holy Spirit. The unholy trinity: Satan, the Antichrist or the Beast, and the False Prophet.

The covenant that the Antichrist or the Beast will make will evidently be a peace covenant, in which he will guarantee Israel's safety in the land. This suggests that Israel will be in her land but will be unable to defend herself for she will have lost any support she may have had previously. Therefore, she will need and welcome the peacemaking role of this head of the confederation of Ten European (Roman) Nations. In offering this covenant, the Antichrist or the ruler will pose as a prince of peace and Israel will accept his authority.[119]

Now, let's talk about the *Great Tribulation* period, which is the last half (or the last three and a half years) of the Tribulation period. Having given a brief overview of the entire Tribulation period prior to His return, Jesus then spoke of the greatest observable sign within that period, the *abomination that causes desolation.* This abomination was spoken of by Daniel (Daniel 9:27). It referred to the disruption of the Jewish worship which will be reinstituted in the Tribulation temple (Daniel 12:11) and the establishment of the worship of the world dictator, the Antichrist, in the temple.[120]

He will make the temple abominable and therefore desolate by setting up in the temple an image of himself to be worshiped (2 Thessalonians 2:4, Revelation 13:14-15). Such an event will be clearly recognized by everyone. When that event occurs, those in Judea should flee to the mountains. They should not be concerned about taking anything with them or returning from the field for possessions, not even for a cloak. The time following this event will be a time of great distress, unequaled from the beginning of the world . . . and never to be equaled again (Jeremiah 30:7).[121]

Christ declares in Matthew 24:21-22, "For then there will be *great tribulation*, such as has not been since the beginning of the world until this time, no, nor ever shall be. And unless those days were shortened, no flesh would be saved; but for the elect's sake those days will be shortened." Christ here clearly identifies this period as the Great Tribulation. It is an intense period of distress and suffering at the end of time.

God's purpose is for the Tribulation period (the seven years) to be a time of judgment though His grace will still be available in the Gospel that will precede Christ's glorious 1,000-year reign in Jerusalem from David's throne.[122]

Let's review. The Tribulation period is seven years. The Antichrist or the Beast will make a covenant with Israel during this seven-year period. The Great Tribulation period begins in the middle of this seven-year covenant, when the Antichrist or the Beast breaks the covenant. "Then he shall confirm a covenant with many for one week; but in the middle of the week he shall bring an end to sacrifice and offering. And on the wing of abominations shall be one who makes desolate, even until the consummation, which is determined, is poured out on the desolate" (Daniel 9:27).

The description of the Great Tribulation given by Christ in answer to the disciples' question is confirmed by additional information in Revelation (see Chapters 6-18). A scroll with seven seals described in Revelation 5:1, is unrolled in Chapter 6. Let's see what happens when these seals are broken.

## THE SEVEN SEAL JUDGMENTS
### Revelation 6

In this chapter, we read of six of these seven *Seal Judgments*. These Seal Judgments include the White Horse, the Red Horse, the Black Horse, the Pale Horse, the Martyrs and the Disaster. The first four of these – the White Horse, the Red Horse, the Black Horse and the Pale Horse – are known as the Four Horsemen of the Apocalypse.

The word *"apocalypse"* means *"revelation."* Let's see what each of these Seal Judgments mean:

1. *The First Seal: The White Horse.* In Revelation 6:2 we read, "And I looked, and behold, *a white horse.* He who sat on it had a bow; and a crown was given to him, and he went out conquering and to conquer." In the Bible, a horse is often used as a symbol of war. For example, at the end of the apocalypse, the Lord Jesus Himself returns on a white horse to settle the issues of Armageddon (Revelation 19:11-16).

2. *The Second Seal: The Red Horse.* In Revelation 6:4 we read, "Another *horse, fiery red,* went out. And it was granted to the one who sat on it to take peace from the earth, and that people should kill one another; and there was given to him a great sword."

3. *The Third Seal: The Black Horse.* In Revelation 6:5 we read, "When He opened the third seal, I heard the third living creature say, 'Come and see.' So I looked, and behold, *a black horse,* and he who sat on it had a pair of scales in his hand." This rider represents famine and economic disaster.

4. *The Fourth Seal: Pale Horse*. In Revelation 6:7-8 we read, "When He opened the fourth seal, I heard the voice of the fourth living creature saying, 'Come and see.' So I looked, and behold, *a pale horse*. And the name of him who sat on it was Death, and Hades followed with him. And power was given to them over a fourth of the earth, to kill with sword, with hunger, with death and by the beasts of the earth." I have heard Bible teachers say that this color of pale is actually a pale green color.

As stated in Chapter 1, as of November 2010, the human population of the world is estimated by the United States Census Bureau to be 6,881,104,426. Now, one fourth of this population would be 1,720,276,106. My friend, that is a lot of people!

5. *The Fifth Seal: Martyrs*. We read in Revelation 6:9, "When He opened the fifth seal, I saw under the altar the souls of those who had been slain for the word of God and for the testimony which they held." Now we are introduced to the first *martyrs* of the Tribulation Period (Matthew 24:9).

These are Jewish believers who go out into the world and preach the Gospel of the kingdom and who are slain for their testimony. The souls that are under the altar are theirs. Let's see what they are saying. "And they cried with a loud voice, saying, "How long, O Lord, holy and true, until You judge and avenge our blood on those who dwell on the earth?" (Revelation 6:10).

6. *The Sixth Seal: Disaster*. Let's read about this in Revelation 6:12-14. "I looked when He opened the sixth seal, and behold, there was a great earthquake; and the sun became black as sackcloth of hair, and the moon became like blood. And the stars of heaven fell to the earth, as a fig tree drops its late figs when it is shaken by a mighty wind. Then the sky receded as a scroll when it is rolled up, and every mountain and island was moved out of its place."

Can you imagine – a great earthquake, the sun becoming black, the moon becoming like blood, the stars falling to the earth, the sky receding as a scroll, and every mountain and island moved out of its place?

Let's see what the kings of the earth, the great men, the rich men, the commanders, the mighty men, every slave, and every free man do. They " . . . hid themselves in the caves and in the rocks of the mountains" (Revelation 6:15).

Why are they hiding? Let's find out in Revelation 6:16-17. "And said to the mountains and rocks, 'Fall on us and hide us from the face of Him who sits on the throne and from the wrath of the Lamb! For the great day of His wrath has come, and who is able to stand?'" The "Lamb" is Jesus Christ. Can you picture this? People hiding in caves and among the rocks of the mountains.

7. *The Seventh Seal – Silence.* It is discussed in Revelation 8:1. "When He opened the seventh seal, there was *silence* in heaven for about half an hour." A silence that is caused by the prayers of God's beleaguered saints on earth.

There are two items of great interest that are to be noted about these prayers:

(1) The postponing of the judgment (Revelation 8:1-4) – God holds up the entire process of judgment while He receives and weighs the prayers of His own.

(2) The precipitating of the judgment (Revelation 8:5-6) – In direct answer to prayer, God acts by setting in motion the trumpet judgments.[123]

The breaking of the seventh seal (8:1) results in the sounding of seven trumpets (8:7-11:15), seven physical judgments in addition to and more severe than those of the first six seals.[124]

## THE SEVEN TRUMPETS
### Revelation 8-9

Now, let's talk about the *Seven Trumpets*.

1. *The First Trumpet: Hail, Fire and Blood.* "The first angel sounded: And *hail and fire followed, mingled with blood,* and they were thrown to the earth. And a third of the trees were burned up, and all green grass was burned up" (Revelation 8:7).

Let's think about this one for a moment. " . . . hail and fire followed, mingled with blood, and they were thrown to the earth." Can you imagine? " . . . And a third of the trees were burned up, and all green grass was burned up." We hear about forest fires in California – but think about this!

2. *The Second Trumpet: Burning Mountain.* "Then the second angel sounded: And something like a *great mountain burning with fire* was thrown into the sea, and a third of the sea became blood. And a third of the living creatures in the sea died, and a third of the ships were destroyed" (Revelation 8:8-9). This would not only decrease man's food supply but reduce his means of obtaining food. We read of a similar time in Exodus 7:14-22.

3. *The Third Trumpet: Star-Wormwood.* "Then the third angel sounded: And a great star fell from heaven, burning like a torch, and it fell on a third of the rivers and on the springs of water. *The name of the star is Wormwood.* A third of the waters became wormwood, and many men died from the water, because it was made bitter" (Revelation 8:10-11).

Revelation 13 lends strong support to the view that the fallen star is Satan himself. He is given the symbolic name of Wormwood (absinth, a bitter and deleterious plant), and he poisons the third part of "the waters," which become bitter and result in the death of many men.[125]

The symbolism of the waters is explained in Revelation 17:15: " . . . *the waters . . . are peoples, multitudes, nations and tongues.*" In other words, Satan's fall to earth results in the immediate poisoning of human life and society. The people of the earth take on the character of the evil one and become "wormwood" too. Satan is bitter because he has been cast out of heaven. Men become bitter and many people die.[126]

4. *The Fourth Trumpet: Cosmic darkness.* "Then the fourth angel sounded: And a third of the sun was struck, a third of the moon, and a third of the stars, so that a third of them were darkened. *A third of the day did not shine, and likewise the night*" (Revelation 8:12).

5. *The Fifth Trumpet: Locusts.* "Then the fifth angel sounded: And I saw a star fallen from heaven to the earth. To him was given the key to the bottomless pit. And he opened the bottomless pit, and smoke arose out of the pit like the smoke of a great furnace. So the sun and the air were darkened because of the smoke of the pit. Then out of the smoke *locusts* came upon the earth. And to them was given power, as the scorpions of the earth have power.

They were commanded not to harm the grass of the earth, or any green thing, or any tree, but only those men who do not have the seal of God on their foreheads. And they were not given authority to kill them, but to torment them for five months. Their torment was like the torment of a scorpion when it strikes a man" (Revelation (9:1-5).

Have you ever been stung by a scorpion? Let's revisit verse 5. " . . . Their torment was like the torment of a scorpion when it strikes a man." The Mayo Clinic Staff identifies the symptoms of a scorpion sting to be difficulty breathing, high blood pressure, increased heart rate, muscle twitching, and weakness. Now, imagine feeling this way and wanting to die – but you cannot.

We read this in Revelation 9:6. "In those days men will seek death and will not find it; they will desire to die, and death will flee from them." Although the sting was not fatal, it inflicted torment that lasted for five months. These locusts probably represent demons which, when released from the pit, took possession of unsaved men and women. This demon possession caused the most intense physical suffering and mental torture.[127]

6. *The Sixth Trumpet: Horsemen.* "Then the sixth angel sounded: And I heard a voice from the four horns of the golden altar which is before God, saying to the sixth angel who had the trumpet, 'Release the four angels who are bound at the great river Euphrates.' So the four angels, who had been prepared for the hour and day and month and year, were released to kill a third of mankind. Now the number of the army of the *horsemen* was two hundred million; I heard the number of them" (Revelation 9:13-16).

The great Euphrates River is important in Scripture. It divides the east and the west. When I read of the Euphrates River, the Sea of Galilee, Jerusalem, Israel and other names of the places in the Bible that correspond with the places in the world, it confirms that God wrote the Bible. Of course, we know that from 2 Timothy 3:16, "All Scripture is given by inspiration of God, and is profitable for doctrine, for reproof, for correction, for instruction in righteousness." What the Bible says will happen – *will happen!*

Furthermore, the Euphrates River was one of the four rivers that flowed out of the garden of Eden. Isn't that awesome?

Where in the Bible is the garden of Eden mentioned? In Genesis. "The Lord God planted a garden eastward in Eden, and there He put the man whom He had formed" (Genesis 2:8). We also get confirmation of the garden of Eden in verse

15, "Then the Lord God took the man and put him in the garden of Eden to tend and keep it."

Let's read Genesis 2:10-11. "Now a river went out of Eden to water the garden, and from there it parted and became four riverheads. The name of the first is the Pishon; it is the one which skirts the whole land of Havilah, where there is gold." Let's read ahead to verses 13-14 of Chapter 2. "The name of the second river is Gihon; it is the one which goes around the whole land of Cush. The name of the third river is Hiddekel; it is the one which goes toward the east of Assyria. The fourth river is the Euphrates."

The Euphrates River is in Genesis, which is the first book of the Bible, as well as in Revelation, which is the last book of the Bible. The Bible is like a puzzle, every book fits together. If you study the book of Genesis, you will see that it is a prerequisite to the understanding of God and His meaning to man.[128]

Let's continue with the *Horsemen*, the sixth Trumpet. We read from Revelation 9:16 that the horsemen numbered 200 million. That is a lot of troops! So, what is their mission? "And thus I saw the horses in the vision: those who sat on them had breastplates of fiery red, hyacinth blue, and sulfur yellow; and the heads of the horses were like the heads of lions; and out of their mouths came fire, smoke and brimstone.

By these three plagues a third of mankind was killed – by the fire and the smoke and the brimstone which came out of their mouths. For in their power is in their mouth and in their tails; for their tails are like serpents, having heads; and with them they do harm" (Revelation 9:17-19).

Let's see what happens to mankind. "But the rest mankind, who were not killed by these plagues, did not repent of the works of their hands, that they should not worship demons, and idols of gold, silver, brass, stone and wood, which can neither see nor hear nor walk. And they did not repent of their murders of their sorceries or their sexual immorality or their thefts" (Revelation 9:20-21).

*They still did not repent.* I can see how this is going to transpire! Can't you? Friend, this will take place! In today's society, people do not want to repent. The word *repent* means *to be sorry for or change ways.*[129] There are people who do not want to go to the Lord Jesus and repent of their sins and ask Him to forgive them. They do not want to say "I am sorry" or "I am wrong." Let's read Luke 5:32. "I have not come to call the righteous, but sinners, to repentance."

God speaks in various ways. He speaks through His Word – the Bible, through Ministers and Believers in Christ (Christians). Listen to what He is saying! What He says, He means! He is serious! He sent His One and Only Son – Jesus – to die on a cross and pay our sin debt so that we would not see His wrath. Will you repent of your sins, ask Him to forgive you and accept Jesus Christ as your Lord and Savior? He loves you so much!

Before the seventh trumpet sounds, let's talk about Chapters 10 and 11 of Revelation. In Chapter 10, we read of "*The Angel and the Little Scroll.*" Let's read verse 7 of this chapter. "But in the days of the sounding of the seventh angel, when he is about to sound, the mystery of God would be finished, as He declared to His servants the prophets."

Let's read of the "*Two Witnesses*" in Revelation 11:3. "And I will give *power* to my *two witnesses*, and they will prophesy one thousand two hundred and sixty days, clothed in sackcloth." Let's continue in verses 5-6, "And if anyone wants to harm them, fire proceeds from their mouth and devours their enemies. And if anyone wants to harm them, he must be killed in this manner. These have power to shut heaven, so that no rain falls in the days of their prophecy; and they have power over waters to turn them to blood, and to strike the earth with all plagues, as often as they desire."

Let's see what happens to these two witnesses. "When they finish their testimony, the beast that ascends out of the bottomless pit will make war against them, overcome them, and kill them" (Revelation 11:7). This beast is the Antichrist. Now these two witnesses are dead. Let's see what happens next. "And their dead bodies will lie in the street of the great city which spiritually is called Sodom and Egypt, where also our Lord was crucified." (Revelation 11:8). The city, which is figuratively Sodom and Egypt, is Jerusalem.

Jerusalem is called Sodom here of its pride, indulgence, prosperous ease, and indifference to the needs of others (see Ezekiel 16:49). And it is called Egypt because of its idolatry, persecution and enslavement to sin and unrighteousness.[130]

Let's see what happens to the dead bodies of these two witnesses. "Then those from the peoples, tribes, tongues, and nations will see their dead bodies three-and-a-half days, and not allow their dead bodies to be put into graves" (Revelation 11:9). The refusal of burial is a great indignity in almost all cultures.

Now, while these two witnesses are dead in the street, let's see what the people on the earth are doing. "And those who dwell on the earth will rejoice over them, make merry, and send gifts to one another, because these two prophets tormented those who dwell on the earth" (Revelation 11:10). Let's look at the beginning of this verse again. "And those who dwell on the earth . . ." This implies some worldwide display. Friend, do you see how this will happen? With Satellite television, you can see the world. All eyes will be focused on this event!

Let's see what happens next. "Now after the three-and-a-half days the breath of life from God entered them, and they stood on their feet, and great fear fell on those who saw them" (Revelation 11:11.) Can you imagine this scene? For three-and-a-half days these two dead bodies laid in the streets.

The people are merry and exchanging gifts when, all of a sudden, God brings the two witnesses back to life and they stand up! The people who saw them were struck with terror. They're alive! They were dead in the streets and now they are alive! I would say that their merriness and exchanging gifts came to a complete halt!

Let's see what happens next. "And they heard a loud voice from heaven saying to them, 'Come up here.' And they ascended to heaven in a cloud, and their enemies saw them" (Revelation 11:12). God vindicated His own. God takes them to heaven as their enemies watched. God is so amazing!

You would think that the people, when they saw these two witnesses alive from being dead, would have repented of their sins and turned to the Lord. However, they did not.

Let's read another story about two men who died and see what happened to each of them. "There was a certain rich man who was clothed in purple and fine linen and fared sumptuously every day. But there was a certain beggar named Lazarus, full of sores, who was laid at his gate, desiring to be fed with the crumbs which fell from the rich man's table. Moreover the dogs came and licked his sores. So it was that the beggar died, and was carried by the angels to Abraham's bosom. The rich man also died and was buried. And being in torments in Hades, he lifted up his eyes and saw Abraham afar off, and Lazarus in his bosom.

"Then he cried and said, 'Father Abraham, have mercy on me, and send Lazarus that he may dip the tip of his finger in water and cool my tongue; for I am tormented in this flame. But Abraham said, 'Son, remember that in your lifetime you received good things, and likewise Lazarus evil things; but now he is comforted and you are tormented. And besides all this, between us and you there is a great gulf fixed, so that those who want to pass from here to you cannot, nor can those from there pass to us.'

"Then he said, 'I beg you therefore, father, that you would send him to my father's house, for I have five brothers, that he may testify to them, lest they also come to this place of torment.' Abraham said to him, 'They have Moses and the prophets; let them hear them. And he said, 'No, father Abraham; but if one goes to them from the dead, they will repent.' But he said to him, 'If they do not hear Moses and the prophets, neither will they be persuaded though one rise from the dead'" Luke 16:19-31.

Let's return to Luke 16:26. "And besides all this, between us and you there is a *great gulf fixed*, so that those who want to pass from here to you cannot, nor can those from there pass to us." The term "gulf" is defined as "a wide gap."[131] Once death has taken place, *that gulf is fixed.* " . . . a great gulf fixed." The word "fixed" means "immovable." There is no passage from heaven to hell or vice versa.

If you *have been* born again, at your death, the Bible says, "We are confident, yes, well pleased rather to be absent from the body and to be present with the Lord" (2 Corinthians 5:8). If you *have not been* born again, at your death the Bible says, "And as it is appointed for men to die once, but after this the judgment" (Hebrews 9:27).

Furthermore, the Bible says, "For He says: 'In an acceptable time I have heard you, and in the day of salvation I have helped you.' Behold, now is the accepted time; behold, *now is the day of salvation*" (2 Corinthians 6:2).

Let's return to Luke 16:22-23. "So it was that the beggar died, and was carried by the angels to Abraham's bosom. The rich man also died and was buried. And being in torments in Hades, he lifted up his eyes and saw Abraham afar off, and Lazarus in his bosom." Notice the beggar died and was carried by the angels to Abraham's bosom. However, the rich man died and he was immediately in Hades (the NIV Bible translation calls it Hell). He was in torment.

Now, let's return to Revelation 11:13 and read what happens after the two witnesses have ascended to heaven. "In the same hour there was a great earthquake, and a tenth of the city fell. In the earthquake seven thousand people were killed, and the rest were afraid and gave glory to the God of heaven."

7. *The Seventh Trumpet: Worship*. "Then the seventh angel sounded: And there were *loud voices in heaven, saying, 'The kingdom of this world have become the kingdoms of our Lord and of His Christ, and He shall reign forever and ever!' And the twenty-four elders who sat before God on their thrones fell on their faces and worshipped God*" (Revelation 11:15-16).

Let's continue with Revelation 13. This chapter deals with the *Beast* and the *False Prophet*. Let's read Revelation 13:5. "And he was given a mouth speaking great things and blasphemies, and he was given authority to continue for forty-two months." These forty-two months are also called the three and one half years period, which is the length of the Great Tribulation period.

The Beast or the Antichrist has four purposes we read in Revelation 13: [132]

(1). *To defy the God of heaven*. "And he was given a mouth speaking great things and blasphemies, and he was given authority to continue for forty-two months. Then he opened his mouth in blasphemy against God, to blaspheme His name, His tabernacle, and those who dwell in heaven" (verses 5-6).

(2). *To destroy the saints of God*. "It was granted to him to make war with the saints and to overcome them. And authority was given him over every tribe, tongue, and nation" (verse 7). The saints here will die rather than submit to him. His rule extends over the entire world, which is the last world empire before Christ's reign. He cannot harm the glorified saints in heaven, but he can harm the believers on earth, at least those not specifically sealed against him.

(3). *To dominate the nations of the earth.* " . . . And authority was given him over every tribe, tongue, and nation" (verse 7).

(4). *To delude the masses of mankind.* "All who dwell on the earth will worship him, whose names have not been written in the Book of Life of the Lamb slain from the foundation of the world. If anyone has an ear, let him hear. He who leads into captivity shall go into captivity; he who kills with the sword must be killed with the sword. Here is the patience and the faith of the saints" (verses 8-10).

Let's read what the False Prophet ordered to be done in his honor in Revelation 13:14-15. "And he deceives those who dwell on the earth by those signs which he was granted to do in the sight of the beast, telling those who dwell on the earth to make an image to the beast who was wounded by the sword and lived. He was granted power to give breath to the image of the beast, that the image of the beast should both speak and cause as many as would not worship the image of the beast to be killed."

Now, let's talk about the *Mark of the Beast.* We read in Revelation 13:16-18, "He causes all, both small and great, rich and poor, free and slave, to receive a *mark* on their right hand or on their foreheads, and that no one may buy or sell except one who has the *mark* or the name of the beast, or the number of his name. Here is wisdom. Let him who has understanding calculate the number of the beast, for it is the number of a man: His number is 666."

The people left on the earth after the Rapture takes place, will be required to take this mark in order to buy or sell. If you take this mark, you are doomed.

To take the mark will signify one's commitment and devotion to the Antichrist, affirming belief by the wearer that Satan, rather than God, is the supreme deity. The mark will be a visible symbol (on the individual) of the immense power and worldwide authority and control of the Antichrist. According to Revelation 20:4, thousands of people will refuse the mark and, as a result, will be beheaded. These Tribulation martyrs will be resurrected at the Second Coming of Christ at the end of the Tribulation period and will reign with Him during the Millennium.[133]

Let's continue with Revelation 14:9-10. "Then a third angel followed them, saying with a loud voice, 'If anyone worships the beast and his image, and receives his mark on his forehead or his hand, he himself shall also drink of the wine of the wrath of God, which is poured out full strength into the cup of His indignation. He shall be tormented with fire and brimstone in the presence of the holy angels and in the presence of the Lamb" (Revelation 14:9-10).

We can fix the time of the third angel's pronouncement as being at the middle of the Tribulation, which is the same as the beginning of the Great Tribulation.[134]

Let's talk more about the number 666. This number is the number of man. Dr. Adrian Rogers wrote, "On the back of your credit cards are magnetic strips that contain information in a series of numbers that can be read by a computer. Soon you will never have to write another check, or keep cash in your billfold or buy a stamp. Let's say every purchase that you make is done by this system."

He continues, "Europe already has a system in place for large corporations to do business this way, and soon it will be the norm for everyone. 'The Universal Product Code on all packaging is one form of this system and your automatic payroll deposit from your job is another. Pretty soon, a person will be able to wave their hand under that light beam at the supermarket, and they will have the proper amount deducted from their account.'"

Furthermore, he says, "In the future, the enforcement of financial obligations will present few difficulties because failure to pay your debts could be disastrous. You could be cut off from your bank cards, making you a non-person, unable to buy or sell."

## THE SEVEN BOWLS
### Revelation 16

At this point, John encounters seven new angels whose responsibility is to dispense the seven bowl judgments, also known as the seven last plagues (15:1). Revelation 15 is a sort of celestial interlude to introduce the pouring out of the seven bowls of divine wrath in Revelation 16.[135]

In Revelation 16, we are going to talk about the Seven Bowl Judgments.

1. *The First Bowl Judgment: Boils.* "So the first went and poured out his bowl upon the earth, and a foul and loathsome sore came upon the men who had the mark of the beast and those who worshiped his image" (Revelation 16:2).

2. *The Second Bowl Judgment: Sea-Blood.* "Then the second angel poured out his bowl on the sea, and it became blood as of a dead man; and every living creature in the sea died" (Revelation 16:3).

3. *The Third Bowl Judgment: Rivers-Blood.* "Then the third angel poured out his bowl on the rivers and springs of water, and they became blood" (Revelation 16:4).

4. *The Fourth Bowl Judgment: Great Heat.* "Then the fourth angel poured out his bowl on the sun, and power was given to him to scorch men with fire. And men were scorched with great heat, and they blasphemed the name of God who has power over these plagues; and they did not repent and give Him glory" (Revelation 16:8-9).

5. *The Fifth Bowl Judgment: Darkness.* "Then the fifth angel poured out his bowl on the throne of the beast, and his kingdom became full of darkness; and they gnawed their tongues because of the pain" (Revelation 16:10).

6. *The Sixth Bowl Judgment: Euphrates River Dried Up.* "Then the sixth angel poured out his bowl on the great river Euphrates, and its water was dried up, so that the way of the kings from the east might be prepared" (Revelation 16:12). Notice that we read of the Euphrates River again.

7. *The Seventh Bowl Judgment: Hail.* "Then the seventh angel poured out his bowl into the air, and a loud voice came out of the temple of heaven, from the throne, saying, 'It is done!' And there were noises and thundering and lightnings; and there was a great earthquake, such a mighty and great earthquake as had not occurred since men were on the earth" (Revelation 16:17-18). We think the earthquakes in California are terrible. Wait till this one takes place. " . . . and there was a great earthquake, such a mighty and great earthquake as had not occurred since men were on the earth. (verse 18)

(Note that the First Trumpet of the Seven Trumpets will occur under the opening of the Seventh Seal. When the Seventh Trumpet sounds, the First Bowl of the Seven Bowls, of the wrath of God, will begin.)

Now let's read Revelation 16:1. "Then I heard a loud voice from the temple saying to the seven angels, 'Go and pour out the bowls of the wrath of God on the earth." Let's ponder this verse. " . . . Go and pour out the bowls of the wrath of God on the earth." His wrath is being poured out of the earth. For you see, my friend, when you are born again, you miss the wrath of God. "Much more then, having now been justified by His blood, we shall be saved from wrath through Him" (Romans 5:9).

Let's go to Genesis for a moment. In Chapters 5-9, we read about a man named Noah. If you recall, God had Noah build an ark. Let's read Genesis 6:11-14. "The earth also was corrupt before God, and the earth was filled with violence. So God looked upon the earth, and indeed it was corrupt, for all flesh had corrupted their way on the earth. And God said to Noah, 'The end of all flesh has come before Me, for the earth is filled with violence through them: and behold, I will destroy them with the earth. Make yourself an ark of gopherwood; make rooms in the ark, and cover it inside and outside with pitch.'"

Let's continue. In Genesis 6:17 we read, "And behold, I Myself am bringing floodwaters on the earth, to destroy from under heaven all flesh in which is the breath of life; everything that is on the earth shall die." Friend, how many people do you think were on the earth at this time? The earth's population, when the flood began, was at least seven billion people.[136] When the flood began, how many people did God save from the flood? He saved Noah and his family on the ark from His wrath. "So Noah, with his sons, his wife, and his sons' wives went into the ark because of the waters of the flood" (Genesis 7:7).

Let's go back for just a moment to Genesis 6:6. "And the Lord was sorry that He had made man on the earth, and *He was grieved in His heart.*" It breaks my heart to know that God was "grieved in his heart." I love Him so much. Does your heart break when God's heart is grieved? Has your heart ever been filled with pain? Have you ever felt grief and sorrow? I have. Sometimes, the hurt and pain can be overwhelming.

This verse says that "He was *grieved* in His heart . . ." The term "grieved" means "to feel sorrow." He created mankind. He loves mankind (see John 3:16). In 2 Peter 3:9 we read, "The Lord is not slack concerning His promise, as some count slackness, but is longsuffering toward us, not willing that any should perish but that all should come to repentance." He doesn't want anyone to perish.

You may ask, "If God loved mankind so, then why did He destroy them in the flood?" God is Holy and He must react against sin. The definition of *holy* is "the pure and loving nature of God separate from evil." God sent His Best – His Son Jesus Christ – to die for our sins. We, as sinners, had to have a perfect sacrifice, who is Jesus.

Therefore, a person has a choice to reject or accept Jesus. "Much more then, having now been justified by His blood, we shall be saved from wrath through Him. For if when we were enemies we were reconciled to God through the death of His Son, much more, having been reconciled, we shall be saved by His life" (Romans 5:9-10).

Let's look at these verses more closely. "Much more then, having now been justified by His blood . . ." The term "justified" in this verse means to be *counted righteous by God*. When we are born again, God sees us as righteous because of our identification by faith with His Son, Jesus.

Let me pause here and say something about salvation. Some people have the misconception that they can be saved whenever they want to. However, let's read John 6:44. "No one can come to Me *unless the Father who sent Me draws him*; and I will raise him up at the last day."

When you are born again, you are saved from the wrath of God, because you are saved through Jesus Christ, who paid for your sin debt on the cross. For you see, God has to judge sin. Therefore, a sinner can be born again and be saved from God's wrath. Or, a sinner can reject Christ and encounter the wrath of God in hell because their sin separates them from God. Heaven is a *perfect* place. There is *no sin* there.

Did you know that if a person is not saved or born again, he or she is an enemy of God? This person is hostile towards the Lord. If a person is left to themselves, they feel no need of being reconciled to Him. Therefore, if a person rejects Jesus Christ as Lord and Savior, he or she is an enemy of God.

Let me ask another question. Does a person seek after God on their own? We find the answer in Romans 3:11. "There is none who understands; there is none who seeks after God." Who seeks after God? There is *none* who seeks after Him.

Let's see what the good news is. "For if when we were enemies we were reconciled to God through the death of His Son, much more, having been reconciled, we shall be saved by His life" (Romans 5:10). As a sinner, we were separated from God. However, when we are born again, we are "reconciled to Him . . ." We are reconciled to God through the death of his Son, Jesus.

Reconciliation is the process by which God and man are reunited. The Bible teaches that God and man are alienated from one another because of God's holiness and man's sinfulness. Although God loves the sinner (Romans 5:8), it is impossible for Him not to judge sin (Hebrews 10:27). Therefore, in biblical reconciliation, both parties are affected. Through the sacrifice of Christ, man's sin is atoned and God's wrath is appeased. Thus, a relationship of hostility and alienation is changed into one of peace and fellowship.[137]

This initiative in reconciliation was taken by God. While we were still sinners and "enemies," Christ died for us (Romans 5:8). Reconciliation is thus God's own completed act, something that takes place before human actions such as confession, repentance, and restitution. God Himself "has reconciled us to Himself through Jesus Christ" (2 Corinthians 5:18). [138]

If Jesus had not died and rose again, we, as sinners, would be without hope. We would all be eternally separated in hell forever. But *He did die, and three days later He arose!* (See Matthew 27 and 28.) Praise His name! He is alive. At this very moment, He is seated on the right hand of God the Father (see Mark 16:19).

Let's return to the Tribulation period and cover one more issue in regards to this period. There will be people born again during this time. However, it will cost them their physical lives. As I have stated earlier, the Antichrist will be ruler during this Tribulation period.

In Revelation 13:7-8 we read, "It was granted to him to make war with the saints and to overcome them. And authority was given him over every tribe, tongue, and nation. All who dwell on the earth will worship him, whose names have not been written in the *Book of Life of the Lamb* slain from the foundation of the world."

Let's talk about Revelation 13:8. "All who dwell on the earth will worship him, whose names have not been written in the Book of Life of the Lamb slain from the foundation of the world."

When a person is saved or born again, his or her name is written in the Lamb's Book of Life. We read in Luke 10:20, "Nevertheless do not rejoice in this, that the spirits are subject to you, *but rather rejoice because your names are written in heaven.*"

Why is it important that *your name* is written in the *Lamb's Book of Life?* We find the answer in Revelation 21:27. "But there shall by no means enter it anything that defiles, or causes an abomination or a lie, *but only those who are written in the Lamb's Book of Life.*" So, who is going to be in heaven? " . . . *But only those who are written in the Lamb's Book of Life.*" Is your name written in the Lamb's Book of Life? Mine is.

Now, let's see what happens if someone's name is not written in the Book of Life. We read in Revelation 20:15, *"And anyone not found written in the Book of Life was cast into the lake of fire."* So, if your name *is not in the Book of Life*, you will be cast into the lake of fire.

Now, let's talk about the *Marriage of the Lamb*. In Revelation 19:7-9 we read, "Let us be glad and rejoice and give Him glory, for the Marriage of the Lamb has come, and

His wife has made herself ready. And to her it was granted to be arrayed in fine linen, clean and bright, for the fine linen is the righteous acts of the saints." You may be wondering, "What is the Marriage of the Lamb"? This event is in heaven and it takes place after the Rapture and prior to the Second Coming of Christ to earth. In this heavenly marriage, Christ is the bridegroom or husband and the church is the bride of Christ.

This wedding will be totally different from all other earthly weddings. First, in an earthly wedding, there can be a last-minute refusal on the part of either the bride or groom. But this cannot happen with the heavenly marriage. The bridegroom has already expressed His great love for his bride (Ephesians 5:25), and He never changes (Hebrews 13:8). And by this time, the heavenly bride has already been glorified and is sinless and therefore cannot be tempted into changing her mind or losing her love for the bridegroom (Ephesians 5:27 and Hebrews 10:14).[139]

Second, in an earthly wedding, a serious legal problem might arise, such as lack of age, or even a previous marriage but not in the heavenly wedding (see Romans 8:33-39). In an earthly wedding the tragedy of death might intervene but not in the heavenly wedding. The bride will never die (John 11:26), nor will the bridegroom (Revelation 1:18).[140]

Let's read Ephesians 5:25-27. "Husbands, love your wives, just as Christ also loved the church and gave Himself for her, that He might sanctify and cleanse her with the washing of water by the word, that He might present her to Himself a glorious church, not having spot or wrinkle or any such thing, but that she should be holy and without blemish."

Following the Marriage of the Lamb is the *Marriage Supper of the Lamb.* Let's read Revelation 19:9. "Then he said to me, 'Write: Blessed are those who are called to the Marriage Supper of the Lamb!' And he said to me, 'These are the true sayings of God.'" What does the Lord call those who are called to the Marriage Supper of the Lamb? He calls them, "Blessed." This "Wedding Supper" will take place in heaven for the bride of Christ, which appears to last seven years during the Tribulation Period.

In my dining room, I have a picture that depicts Jesus' hands open and below them is a long banquet table fully set, with plates, napkins, and glasses. At the top is "The Invitation" and "RSVP."

Have you ever received an invitation to an event and had to RSVP? "RSVP" is from the French, "Repondez s'il vous plait," which means "reply please" or "please respond."[141] Likewise, have you made preparations to be at the Marriage Supper of the Lamb? I would hate for you to miss it.

Now, let's talk about the *Second Coming of Christ.* In Revelation 19:11-13 we read, "Now I saw heaven opened, and behold, a white horse. And He who sat on him was called Faithful and True, and in righteousness He judges and makes war. His eyes were like a flame of fire, and on His head were many crowns. He had a name written that no one knew except Himself. He was clothed with a robe dipped in blood, and His name is called The Word of God."

Who is this Person? My Lord and Savior, Jesus Christ. He is on the white horse. What is this event? The glorious Second Coming of Christ to earth in order to take care of His enemies and set up His Kingdom. I get so excited when I read the book of Revelation. It represents the future.

Let's read Revelation 1:3. "*Blessed* is he who reads and those who hear the words of this prophecy, and keep those things which are written in it; for the time is near." A person is *blessed* if they read Revelation. We read this again in Revelation 22:7. "Behold, I am coming quickly! *Blessed* is he who keeps the words of the prophecy of this book."

The Second Coming of Christ, which is when Jesus Christ comes to the earth with His saints, is not the same as the Rapture. The Rapture is when Jesus Christ comes in the air for

His saints. In His Second Coming, Jesus will bodily return to earth just as He bodily went to heaven at His ascension.

Let's read Zechariah 14:4. "And in that day His feet will stand on the Mount of Olives, which faces Jerusalem on the east. And the Mount of Olives shall be split in two, from east to west, making a very large valley; half of the mountain shall move toward the north and the half of it toward the south."

Likewise, let's read another passage in the Bible that mentions the Second Coming of Christ. In Matthew 24:30 we read, "Then the sign of the Son of Man will appear in heaven, and then all the tribes of the earth will mourn, and they will see the Son of Man coming on the clouds of heaven with power and great glory."

Guess who else will be with Jesus on His return to the earth? I will be, for one – all the saints – those who are born again. We, as believers in Jesus are included in the armies of heaven. Let's read Revelation 19:14. "And the armies in heaven, clothed in fine linen, white and clean, followed Him on white horses." That *should* excite you if you are born again! Just imagine Jesus Christ leading the way on a white horse. On His robe and on His thigh, He has the name written:

## *"KING OF KINGS AND LORD OF LORDS"*

We, who are born again (the saints), are behind Him, on white horses. Guess what we will be dressed in? Fine linen, white and clean. Go, Lord Jesus, go! What a day that will be! Furthermore, the Second Coming will be a time of the gathering of all the elect – those resurrected, those translated, and even those in their natural bodies on the earth. All participate in one way or another in this dramatic event related to the Second Coming.[142]

What is the stated purpose of the Second Coming? Let's read Psalm 96:13 to find the answer. "For He is coming, for He is coming to judge the earth. He shall judge the world with righteousness, and the peoples with His truth."

In concurrence with the Second Coming of Christ, the *Battle of Armageddon*, which is the last great world war of history, will take place in Israel. This battle is described in Daniel 11:40-45, Joel 3:9-17, Zechariah 14-1-3 and Revelation 16:14-16.

Let's read Revelation 16:14-16. "For they are spirits of demons, performing signs, which go out to the kings of the earth and of the whole world, to gather them to the battle of that day of God Almighty. Behold, I am coming as a thief. Blessed is he who watches, and keeps his garments, lest he walk naked and they see his shame. And they gathered them together to the place called in Hebrew, *Armageddon*."

According to the Bible, great armies from the east and the west will gather and assemble on this plain. The Antichrist will defeat armies from the south who would threaten his power, and he will destroy a revived Babylon in the east before turning his forces toward Jerusalem to subdue and destroy it. As he and his armies move upon Jerusalem, God will intervene and Jesus Christ will return to rescue His people Israel. The Lord and His angelic army will destroy the armies, capture the Antichrist and the False Prophet, and cast them into the Lake of Fire (Revelation 19:11-21).[143]

The Battle of Armageddon will be the conclusion of the Antichrist's reign and will end with the Second Coming of Jesus Christ, who will destroy the Antichrist and his armies.

Let's see what happens then. After the Battle of Armageddon, there will be peace for a thousand years. These thousand years represent the *Millennium*.

The word "millennium" comes from the Latin word "mille," meaning one thousand, and "annum," meaning year. The Greek word "chilias" which also means one thousand, appears six times in Revelation 20, defining the duration of Christ's kingdom before the destruction of the old heaven and the old earth. Therefore, the *Millennium* refers to one thousand years of Christ's future reign of earth, which will immediately precede eternity (Ryrie, pages 145-146). During the Millennium, Christ will reign in time and space.[144]

Friend, remember that during this thousand years reign of Christ, Satan is bound. He is not on the earth. "He laid hold of the dragon, that serpent of old, who is the Devil and Satan, and bound him for a thousand years; and he cast him into the bottomless pit, and shut him up, and set a seal on him, so that he should deceive the nations no more till the thousand years were finished. But after these things he must be released for a little while" (Revelation 20:2-3).

Let's see what happens after the thousand years and when Satan is released. "Now when the thousand years have expired, Satan will be released from his prison and will go out to deceive the nations which are in the four corners of the earth, *Gog and Magog,* to gather them together to battle, whose number is as the sand on the sea" (Revelation 20:7-8).

Then, we come to the *Great White Throne Judgment.* This judgment is for the unsaved only. Let's read Hebrews 9:27. "And as it is appointed for men to die once, but after this the judgment." Immediately following the Rapture, the believer will stand before the *Judgment Seat of Christ* (see 2 Corinthians 5:10). However, the unbeliever or unsaved will be at the Great White Throne Judgment.

Let's see what happens next. "And I saw the dead, small and great, standing before God, and books were opened. And another book was opened, which is the Book of Life. And the dead were judged according to their works, by the things which were written in the books" (Revelation 20:12).

"The dead, small and great" refers to those who have lived throughout history and, regardless of their stature or position, died without acknowledging and accepting Jesus Christ's payment for their sins.[145]

Let's continue with Revelation 20:13. "The sea gave up the dead who were in it, and Death and Hades delivered up the dead who were in them. And they were judged, each one according to his works." They will be judged according to their works. Picture this: The books have now been read; no one is speaking, and *all* the people at the Great White Throne Judgment are found guilty before God.

What is the judgment? We find the answer in Revelation 20:15. "And anyone not found written in the Book of Life was cast into the lake of fire." Let's see what the Lord will tell them. "Then He will also say to those on the left hand, 'Depart from Me, you cursed, into the everlasting fire prepared for the devil and his angels'" (Matthew 25:41).

Let's look at what the lake of fire is. We read in Matthew 8:12. "But the sons of the kingdom will be cast out into outer darkness. There will be weeping and gnashing of teeth." Also, let's read Mark 9:48. "Where 'their worm does not die, and the fire is not quenched.'"

The worm (internal torment) and the not quenched (external torment) (quoted from the LXX of Isaiah 66:24) vividly portrays the unending, conscious punishment that awaits all who refuse God's salvation. The essence of hell is unending torment and eternal exclusion from His present.[146]

Let me take a moment and say the place called *hell* is not a place where fun and games will take place. Some people have the misconception that they will be partying in hell. Let's read what will take place in hell. Let's read Matthew 8:12. " . . . There will be *weeping and gnashing of teeth*."

Jesus came to take our punishment so that we would not go to hell. There are *only* two places that a person will go when he or she dies: *heaven or hell*. Let's read in Luke 16:22-23 about hell. "So it was that the beggar died, and was carried by the angels to Abraham's bosom. The rich man also died and was buried. And *being in torments in Hades*, he lifted up his eyes and saw Abraham afar off, and Lazarus in his bosom." Was the rich man in torment in hell? Yes. Actually, verse 23 said that he was in *torments* not just torment. What does the word "torment" mean? It means "a state of great bodily or mental suffering, agony, and misery."[147]

Let's take a moment and read a story told by evangelist Ronnie Hill.

> *A teenage boy had just gotten his driver's license and was so excited about driving his car. His mom was in the kitchen cooking dinner. He came in and said, "Mom, I will go to the grocery store. What do you need?" She said, "Son, I don't need anything, thanks for asking."*
>
> *A few minutes later, the son came back into the kitchen and said, "Mom, let me go to the dry cleaners and pick up the clothes." She said, "Son, your dad is going there on his way home from work." He came back in for the third time, "Mom, maybe I need to go to the post office and mail something for you." She said, "Son, we use that box at the end of the driveway to mail our letters." Finally, she thought if he comes back in here, I will let him go get some milk. Well, sure enough, he came back into the kitchen. The mom said, "Son, go to the grocery store and get some milk and come straight home." She knew that he must really want to drive his car. So, he grabbed the keys and she said, "Come straight home."*
>
> *He took off and went to the store and got the milk. He came straight home but decided to go real slow in front of his friend's house so they could see him driving. When he got to Main Street, he decided to adjust the radio station from the oldies to something else. In the meantime, he was going 55 mph in a 30 mph speed zone. Suddenly, he hears sirens behind*

*him. He pulls over and the policeman walks up to his car. He said, "Son, do you know how fast you were going?" He said, "No, sir, I don't." The policeman said, "You were driving 55 mph in a 30 mph speed zone. You will need to go to the courthouse and appear before the judge because you were exceeding the posted speed limit." So, the teenager followed him to the courthouse.*

*While the teenager is standing in the courthouse waiting on the judge, the judge comes out and asks the teenager, "Son, you were caught driving 55 mph in a 30 mph speed zone, do you understand?" The teenager said, "Yes Sir I do." The judge said, "When you break the law, you have to pay the fine. The fine for your breaking the law is either a $300.00 fine or 30 days in jail."*

*The teenager said to the judge, "I don't have $300.00." The judge said, "You know that the penalty is $300 or 30 days in jail." The teenager repeated, "But, I don't have $300.00." The judge, who was his dad, walked down to his son and said, "Son, as a judge I cannot help you, you broke the law. However as your dad, I can pay your fine."*

Friend, we have a fine that we cannot pay. Jesus came to this earth to die on a cross to pay our fine, our sin debt. "For the wages of sin is death, but the gift of God is eternal life in Christ Jesus our Lord" (Romans 6:23). Eternal life is in Jesus Christ.

Let's return to our discussion of hell. We read in Mark 9:48. "Where their worm does not die, and the fire is not quenched." Hell is dark. People will be weeping and gnashing their teeth. You may ask how long this will go on. This will continue throughout eternity – forever.

I remember 9/11, when the Twin Towers were on fire. Sadly, people were jumping out of the windows to their deaths to escape the flames. Have you ever stood close to a fire? It gets really hot. If a person's name is not written in the Book of Life, he or she will be thrown into a lake of fire. "And anyone not found written in the Book of Life was cast into the lake of fire" (Revelation 20:15).

Let me reiterate what the Book of Life is. The Book of Life is a heavenly book in which the names of the righteous – the redeemed or saved – are written.[148]

# CHAPTER 6

## *JESUS CHRIST: THE DOOR INTO HEAVEN*

Many people believe that they know how to get into heaven. Some people believe that their good behavior will get them into heaven. But if this were the case, Jesus Christ would not have died. Let's read Isaiah 64:6. "But we are all like an unclean thing, and all our righteousnesses are like filthy rags; we all fade as a leaf, and our iniquities, like the wind, have taken us away."

In 1994, a large symposium on the religions of the world met in Chicago. It was attended by over seven thousand representatives from every major religion in the world. Irwin Lutzer, who was the pastor of Chicago's Moody Church, attended that symposium in person and described the experience:

> *I walked through the display area in search of a sinless prophet/teacher/Savior. I asked a Hindu Swami whether any of their teachers claimed sinlessness. "No" he said, appearing irritated with my question, "if anyone claims he is sinless, he is not a Hindu!"*
>
> *What about Buddha? No, I was told, he didn't claim sinlessness. He found a group of ascetics and preached sermons to them. He taught that all outward things are only*

distractions and encouraged a life of discipline and contemplation. He sought enlightenment and urged his followers to do the same. He died seeking enlightenment. No sinlessness here.

What about Baha ullah? He claimed he had a revelation from God that was more complete, more enlightened than those before him. Though he was convinced of the truth of his teaching, he made few personal claims. He thought his writings were "more perfect" than others, but he never claimed perfection or sinlessness for himself.

When I came to the representatives of the Muslim faith, I already knew that in the Koran the prophet Mohammed admitted he was in need of forgiveness. They agreed. "There is one God, Allah and Mohammed is His prophet" is the basic Muslim creed. But Mohammed was not perfect. Again, no sinlessness there.

Why was I searching for a sinless Savior? Because I don't want to have to trust a Savior who is in the same predicament as I am. I can't trust my eternal soul to someone who is still working through his own imperfections. Since I'm a sinner, I need someone who is standing on higher ground.

Understandably, none of the religious leaders I spoke with even claimed to have a Savior. Their prophets, they said, showed the way but made no pretense to be able to personally forgive sins or transform so much as a single human being. Like a street sign, they gave directions but were not able to take us where we need to go; if we need any saving, we will have to do it ourselves.

> *The reason is obvious: No matter how wise,*
> *no matter how gifted, no matter how influential*
> *other prophets, gurus, and teachers might be,*
> *they had the presence of mind to know that*
> *they were imperfect just like the rest of us. They*
> *never even presumed to be able to reach down*
> *into the murky water of human depravity and*
> *bring sinners into the presence of God. How*
> *different was Christ! Only Christianity can*
> *offer forgiveness of sins through the shed blood*
> *of Jesus Christ and eternal salvation through*
> *faith in Him.*[149]

Jesus Christ is the perfect and sinless Son of God. He died and bore our sins on Himself to save us from eternal separation from God.

Let's read Ephesians 2:8-9. "For by grace you have been saved through faith, and that not of yourselves; it is the gift of God, not of works, lest anyone should boast." Let's look closer at this verse. "For by *grace* you have been saved . . ." Grace is favor or kindness given to us despite the fact that we do not deserve it. We are not worthy to be saved because we are sinners, but it is by God's grace. " . . . through *faith* . . ."

Let's consider what faith is. "Now *faith* is *the substance of things hoped for, the evidence of things not seen*" (Hebrews 11:1). Faith is when a person takes his or her place as a guilty and lost sinner and receives the Lord Jesus as their Lord and Savior as their *only* hope of salvation.

Let's return to Ephesians 2:8-9. " . . . And that not of yourselves" – a person does not deserve nor can they earn salvation – " . . . it is the gift of God . . ." – salvation is a free and unconditional gift from God. *It is the only way God offers salvation.* It is free, but it cost Jesus Christ His life.

"Not of works, lest anyone should boast." It is not something a person can earn through baptism, church membership, church attendance, holy communion, trying to keep the Ten Commandments, giving to charities, being good or being raised in a Christian home. It is not about a *religion* but through having a personal *relationship* with Jesus Christ.

The *only way* for you to enter into heaven is through *"The Door "*– Jesus Christ and Him alone. When you are born again, your name is written in the Lamb's Book of Life. "But there shall by no means enter it anything that defiles, or causes an abomination or a lie, *but only those who are written in the Lamb's Book of Life"* (Revelation 21:27).

Before we leave this discussion of how a person enters into heaven, let's see whose citizenship is in heaven. We read in Philippians 3:20. "For our citizenship is in heaven, from which we also eagerly wait for the Savior, the Lord Jesus Christ." Whose citizenship is in heaven? The people whose citizenship is in heaven are those of us who have been born again.

# CHAPTER 7

## *JESUS CHRIST: THE CREATOR OF HEAVEN*

I get so excited about going on vacation to new places. When our boys were young, Rick and I took them on a three-week vacation – the "Y2K" trip. We flew to San Francisco. There we rented a van, and our first stop was Muir Woods. I remember how tall the redwood trees were. Then we went on to Yosemite National Park to stay at a bed and breakfast. The first thing out of the boys' mouths was, "No TV? What are we going to do?" Well, they rode their first and probably only horse there. The next stop was Lake Tahoe. It was absolutely stunning! The water was so deep blue it reminded me of Aruba. The grass and trees were so green, and the sky was just beautiful. It was so peaceful.

Then, we went on to the Grand Tetons. They are grand! The beautiful Lake Jenny glistening in front of the snow-capped mountains off in the distance. God's creation is absolutely magnificent!

Following the Grand Tetons, we went to the Yellowstone National Park and saw the geysers, the natural hot springs that periodically eject a blast of water into the air.

Then my husband decides that he wants to touch a geyser. It has to be a man thing! So, the one that he decides to touch is called the "Solitary Geyser." It erupts about four feet every five to seven minutes. I have a photo of him squatting down touching this boiling water. Now, if he wants to touch it, that is his business. But, then he wants me to touch it. He said, "It really wasn't bad. Try it, Lisa." No way. I have no desire to be hit by a boiling geyser, much less touch one.

Then we go on to see Old Faithful, a cone geyser. It was named in 1870 and was the first geyser in the park to receive a name. When we get to Old Faithful, it was barely spewing so we said it was "temporarily out of order." However, it did spew. It was amazing. The eruptions of Old Faithful shoot 3,700 to 8,400 gallons of boiling water to a height of 106 to 185 feet lasting from one and a half to five minutes.

A couple of other places that intrigued me on this trip were Pike's Peak and the Grand Canyon. Because of Pike's Peak's high elevation, some people can get light-headed from the lack of oxygen. The Grand Canyon was absolutely astonishing. Again, our God has created some beautiful places on this earth.

I feel blessed to have seen a lot of places in the United States and some international. But I just love Tennessee, which is where I live. It has the most beautiful days. The blue sky with white cotton clouds and the beautiful green grass. Let's not forget the mountains. Sometimes I get blessed and see a hummingbird, which I truly think are adorable. I may even see from our sunroom a deer or two in the yard. Then at dusk, sometimes when I look at the sky it looks like God has taken a paintbrush and put swishes of pink and red on it. When I think of the sky, the mountains, the hummingbirds, and the deer, I think how awesome is our God!

Now let's talk about the most beautiful place yet to come – *heaven*. My dad's favorite song is "How Beautiful Heaven Must Be." It will be beautiful!

The King James Version of the Bible employs the word "heaven" 582 times in 550 different verses. The Hebrew word usually translated "heaven," *shamayim*, is a plural noun form that literally means "the heights." The Greek word translated "heaven" is "ouranos" (the same word that inspired the name of the planet Uranus). It refers to that which is raised up or lofty. Scripture uses both "shamayim" and "ouranos" to refer to three different places.[150]

Let's begin by stating, as previously mentioned, who created heaven. Let's read in John 14:1-3, "Let not your heart be troubled; you believe in God, believe also in Me. In My Father's house are many mansions; if it were not so, I would have told you. *I go to prepare a place for you.* And if I go and prepare a place for you, I will come again and receive you to Myself; that where I am, there you may be also." *Who is going to prepare a place for the people who are saved or born again? Jesus Christ.*

Let's look again at John 14:2. "In My Father's house are many mansions; if it were not so, I would have told you. I go to prepare a place for you." "I go to prepare a place for you" may have two meanings. The Lord Jesus went to Calvary to prepare a place for His own. It is through His atoning death that believers in Christ are assured a place there. But also the Lord went back to heaven to prepare a place. We do not know very much about this place, but we know that provision is being made for every child of God "a prepared place for a prepared people!"[151]

Let's continue reading in Revelation 21:1-3. "Now I saw a *new heaven and a new earth*, for the first heaven and the first earth had passed away. Also there was no more sea. Then I, John, saw the *holy city, New Jerusalem, coming down out of heaven from God*, prepared as a bride adorned for her husband. And I heard a loud voice from heaven saying, 'Behold, the tabernacle of God is with men, and He will dwell with them, and they shall be His people. God Himself will be with them and be their God.'"

It is a *new heaven and a new earth*. The word "new" means not merely new as to time but also as to kind. It is a new kind of heaven and a new kind of earth, proof of which is found in the fact that the new earth will have no sea. The first heaven and the first earth are not to be annihilated; they are to be purged by fire and regenerated. Satan has defiled both spheres, and God will therefore make them anew. They are made new in the same sense that the believer is "a new man" in Christ, that is, he is a changed man, quickened and renewed by the Spirit of God.[152]

Let's talk about the *holy city, New Jerusalem, coming down out of heaven from God.* This is a literal city, the great heavenly capital of the renewed earth, throughout the Millennium, and the enduring home of the saints for all eternity. John later gives a detailed description of this city and tells us of its glories and its relationship to the millennial earth.[153]

Let's not confuse the earthly Jerusalem with the heavenly Jerusalem. The earthly Jerusalem will be the capital city of the nations during the Millennium. The heavenly Jerusalem will be the home of the saints during the Millennium and for all eternity. [154]

Let's read Hebrews 11:16. "But now they desire a better, that is, a heavenly country. Therefore God is not ashamed to be called their God, for He has prepared a city for them."

I like what John Phillips wrote. "We shall feel as much at ease and at home in heaven as we do on earth right now. Heaven contains much with which we are fondly familiar.[155]

Let's continue. Will there be crying, mourning, death, or pain in heaven? No. "And God will wipe away every tear from their eyes; there shall be no more death, nor sorrow, nor crying. There shall be no more pain, for the former things have passed away" (Revelation 21:4). Imagine that! No more crying, no more mourning, no more death and no more pain. Life on earth is hard. People get really sick. People lose their loved ones in death. People lose their jobs. Most people struggle with something in their lives. In heaven, which is only for those who are saved, there will be none of those things!

Let's see what we will be doing in heaven. We will never grow bored! We will sing (Revelation 15:3-5). Those who could never carry a tune on earth will be able to sing in heaven and never grow weary of exalting the name of the King of Kings. We will serve perfectly, enabled by the power that is able to conform all things to the pleasure of His sovereign will (Revelation 1:1; 7:3; 10:7; 11:18; 15:3; 19:5; 22:6). We will share unbroken fellowship (Revelation 19:9, Hebrews 12:22-24) with angels, members of the Church, God, Jesus, and the spirits of just men made perfect. Never again will we have to say goodbye to a loved one.[156]

God will have different things for different people to do. God made each of us unique with a special ministry and responsibility. Each of us in our own right has a purpose and design for what God has called us to do. There are many distinct groups in heaven, all unique in their responsibility before God. For instance, the twenty-four elders are crowned, enthroned, and seated (Revelation 4:10; 11:16). The 144,000 from the Tribulation period have no crowns or thrones and are standing up and singing a song that no one else knows (Revelation 14:3).[157]

Let's see what heaven will look like. We read in Revelation 21:11-13, "Having the glory of God. Her light was like a most precious stone, like a jasper stone, clear as crystal. Also she had a great and high wall with twelve gates, and twelve angels at the gates, and names written on them, which are the names of the twelve tribes of the children of Israel: three gates on the east, three gates on the north, three gates on the south, and three gates on the west." It will be brightly shining.

Let's see what the great and high wall is made of. "The construction of its wall was of jasper; and the city was pure gold, like clear glass" (Revelation 21:18). In downtown Chattanooga, there is a building that looks like gold. It stands out from the other buildings. I can only imagine a city of pure gold.

Let's continue. "Now the wall of the city had twelve foundations, and on them were the names of the twelve apostles of the Lamb" (Revelation 21:14). In Revelation 21:19-20, we read of a description of its foundations. "The foundations of the wall of the city were adorned with all kinds of precious stones: the first foundation was jasper, the second sapphire, the third chalcedony, the fourth emerald, the fifth sardonyx, the sixth sardius, the seventh chrysolite, the eighth beryl, the ninth topaz, the tenth chrysoprase, the eleventh jacinth, and the twelfth amethyst."

Now, let's look at some of the stone colors in the foundation. The sapphire stone is a deep royal blue, the emerald stone is bright green, the sardonyx stone is red and white, the chrysolite stone is golden, the beryl stone is sea green, the jacinth stone is red purple or violet, and the amethyst stone is purple. Can you just imagine? How beautiful!

Let's see the description of the twelve gates. "The twelve gates were twelve pearls: each individual gate was of one pearl. And the street of the city was pure gold, like transparent glass" (Revelation 21:21). A street made of pure gold, like transparent glass. Think about it!

Let's see what is proceeding from the throne of God and the Lamb. "And he showed me a pure river of water of life, clear as crystal, proceeding from the throne of God and of the Lamb" (Revelation 22:1).

Now, let's look at what is on either side of this river. "In the middle of its street, and on either side of the river, was the tree of life, which bore twelve fruits, each tree yielding its fruit every month. The leaves of the tree were for the healing of the nations" (Revelation 22:2).

Let's look at the measurements of this city. "The city is laid out as a square; its length is as great as its breadth. And he measured the city with the reed: twelve thousand furlongs. Its length, breadth, and height are equal. Then he measured its wall: one hundred and forty-four cubits, according to the measure of a man, that is, of an angel" (Revelation 21:16-17). The city is 12,000 stadia in length and width, approximately 1,400 miles on each side.

Tremendous as is the dimension of the city, the amazing fact is that it is also 1,400 miles high.[158]

Let's see whose citizenship will be there. Let's read Philippians 3:20. "For our citizenship is in heaven, from which we also eagerly wait for the Savior, the Lord Jesus Christ." Those who have been born again are the ones whose names are written in the Lamb's Book of Life. They will be in heaven.

Let's see who will not be there. "But there shall by no means enter it anything that defiles, or causes an abomination or a lie, but only those who are written in the Lamb's Book of Life" (Revelation 21:27).

Let's see who else will be there. " . . . *the throne of God and of the Lamb shall be in it*, and His servants will serve Him" (Revelation 22:3).

Let's see if there will be night. "There shall be no night there: They need no lamp nor light of the sun, for the Lord God gives them light. And they shall reign forever and ever" (Revelation 22:5). I don't know about you, but I like the light over the dark.

This is most of the description given in Revelation of this holy city, the New Jerusalem. We know from Revelation 21:10 that John saw this holy city, which many of us believe to be heaven. I also believe there is much about heaven that the Lord God Almighty and the Lamb has prepared for those of us who are born again, that when we get there, it will take our breath away!

Let's read 1 Corinthians 2:9. "But as it is written: 'Eye has not seen, nor ear heard, nor have entered into the heart of man the things which God has prepared for those for love Him.'"

Oh dearest one, my prayer is that you will come to know my sweet Lord and Savior – Jesus Christ. He loves you so much! I pray that Jesus Christ will be your "Door" to heaven.

As I conclude, my objective was to biblically prove why Jesus Christ is the only Door to heaven. It has been proven!

Thank you for taking the time to read this book. My prayer is that if you have not already made the commitment to trust Jesus Christ as your Lord and Savior, you will. For you see – *He is the One and Only Door to Heaven!*

# ONE SOLITARY LIFE

He was born in an obscure village
The child of a peasant woman
He grew up in another obscure village
Where He worked in a carpenter shop
Until He was thirty

He never wrote a book
He never held an office
He never went to college
He never visited a big city
He never travelled more than two hundred miles
From the place where He was born
He did none of the things
Usually associated with greatness
He had no credentials but Himself

He was only thirty three

His friends ran away
One of them denied Him
He was turned over to His enemies
And went through the mockery of a trial
He was nailed to a cross between two thieves

While dying, His executioners gambled for His clothing
The only property He had on earth

When He was dead
He was laid in a borrowed grave
Through the pity of a friend

Nineteen centuries have come and gone
And today Jesus is the central figure of the human race

And the leader of mankind's progress
All the armies that have ever marched
All the navies that have ever sailed
All the parliaments that have ever sat
All the kings that ever reigned put together
Have not affected the lift of mankind on earth
As powerfully as that One Solitary Life.
~ Dr. James Allen (1926)

*I am THE DOOR, If anyone enters by Me, he will be saved, and will go in and out and find pasture"*
*(John 10:19).*

*Have you opened your heart to "THE DOOR?"*

# ENDNOTES

1   Dr. Charles Swindoll, *Jesus: The Greatest Life of All.* (Nashville: Thomas Nelson, 2008) vii-viii.
2   Herbert Lockyer, Sr. *Nelson's Illustrated Bible Dictionary.* (Nashville: Thomas Nelson, 1986) 905.
3   Lockyer, 905.
4   J. Dwight Pentecost, *The Words & Works of Jesus Christ.* (Grand Rapids: Zondervan Corporation, 1981) 294-295.
5   Lockyer, 232.
6   Lockyer, 62-63.
7   William MacDonald, *Believer's Bible Commentary.* (Nashville: Thomas Nelson, 1980) 1697-1698.
8   MacDonald, 1698.
9   MacDonald, 1698.
10  John Phillips, *Exploring Romans: An Expository Commentary.* (Grand Rapids: Kregel Publications, 2002) 69-70.
11  Luke 23:39-43 (The New Scofield Reference Bible - Authorized King James Version). Commentary.
12  MacDonald, 1303.
13  MacDonald, 1303.
14  Erwin W. Lutzer, *Seven Reasons Why You Can Trust The Bible.* (Chicago: Moody Press, 1998) 32.
15  Lockyer, 316.
16  Abridged from United States Earthquakes, 1960
17  Wikipedia, The Free Encyclopedia
18  www.definitions.net
19  Lockyer, 869.
20  Lockyer, 869.

21    Lockyer, 869.
22    Lockyer, 370.
23    Lockyer, 347.
24    John Phillips, *Exploring Hebrews: An Expository Commentary.*
      (Grand Rapids: Kregel Publications, 2002) 104.
25    MacDonald, 153.
26    Benjamin Galan & Brent Ashby, *Rose Guide to the
      Tabernacle.* (Torrance: Bristol Works Inc, 2008) 65.
27    Webster's Dictionary
28    MacDonald, 1979.
29    Hannah Whitall Smith, *Perfect Peace* (Chicago: Moody
      Press, 2000) 10.
30    Joyce Meyers, *Help Me I'm Worried* (Tulsa, Oklahoma:
      Harrison House, 1998) 25-26.
31    MacDonald, 1466.
32    John F. Walvoord & Roy B. Zuck, *The Bible Knowledge
      Commentary: New Testament.* (Colorado Springs: Chariot
      Victor Publishing, 1983) 673.
33    Tim LaHaye & Ed Hinson, *The Popular Encyclopedia of Bible
      Prophecy.* (Eugene: Harvest House Publishers, 2004) 367.
34    Tim LaHaye, *Jesus, Who is He?* (Colorado Springs:
      Multnomah Books, 1996) 127.
35    Henry M. Morris, *The Genesis Record.* (Grand Rapids:
      Baker Book House, 1976)
36    Dr. Charles F. Stanley, *The Charles F. Stanley's Life
      Principles Bible.* (Nashville, Thomas Nelson, Inc., 2005)
      1.
37    John F. Walvoord & Roy B. Zuck, *The Bible Knowledge
      Commentary: Old Testament.* (Colorado Springs: Chariot
      Victor Publishing, 1985) 818.
38    MacDonald, 36.
39    MacDonald, 36.
40    MacDonald, 36.
41    Lockyer, 610.
42    Greene, 22.

43  Greene, 22.

44  Greene, 22.

45  Stanley, Sermon Outline, www.intouch.org

46  MacDonald, 36.

47  MacDonald, 36.

48  Henry Clarence Thiessen, *Lectures In Systematic Theology*. (Grand Rapids: William B. Eeerdmans Publishing Company, 1949) 211-215

49  MacDonald, 1371.

50  Walvoord & Zuck, *The Bible Knowledge Commentary: New Testament*, 20.

51  Walvoord & Zuck, *The Bible Knowledge Commentary: New Testament*, 20.

52  Walvoord & Zuck, *The Bible Knowledge Commentary: New Testament*, 20.

53  Walvoord & Zuck, *The Bible Knowledge Commentary: New Testament*, 20.

54  Walvoord & Zuck, *The Bible Knowledge Commentary: New Testament*, 208.

55  Lockyer, 1017.

56  MacDonald, 1374.

57  Dr. Anthony Pezzotta, *Truth Encounter*. (Foreign Mission Board, SBC., 1996) 133.

58  Walvoord & Zuck, *The Bible Knowledge Commentary: New Testament*, 209.

59  Lockyer, 889.

60  Lockyer, 556.

61  MacDonald, 1376.

62  MacDonald, 1376.

63  MacDonald, 1376.

64  MacDonald, 1376.

65  MacDonald, 1376.

66  MacDonald, 1378.

67  Walvoord & Zuck, *The Bible Knowledge Commentary: New Testament*, 212.

68 Pentecost, 93.

69 J. W. Shepherd, *The Christ of the Gospels*. (Grand Rapids: William B. Eerdmans, 1946) 71.

70 Shepherd, 71.

71 Pentecost, 94.

72 Pentecost, 94.

73 Pentecost, 94.

74 MacDonald, 2003-2004.

75 MacDonald, 1212.

76 Lockyer, 798.

77 Lockyer, 800.

78 Lockyer, 800.

79 Lockyer, 558.

80 Pentecost, 462-463.

81 MacDonald, 1307.

82 Lockyer, 267.

83 Lockyer, 267.

84 MacDonald, 1309.

85 MacDonald, 1310.

86 Lockyer, 249.

87 Pentecost, 500.

88 Thiessen, 243.

89 Thiessen, 243-244.

90 Thiessen, 244.

91 Thiessen, 247.

92 Thiessen, 248.

93 Thiessen, 248.

94 Thiessen, 248.

95 Lockyer, 107.

96 MacDonald, 1713.

97 MacDonald, 2180.

98 Lewis Sperry Chafer & John F. Walvoord, *Major Bible Themes*. (Grand Rapids: Zondervan Publishing House, 1974) 72-74.

99 Chafer & Walvoord, 72.

100 Chafer & Walvoord, 72.

101 Chafer & Walvoord, 73.

102 Chafer & Walvoord, 73-74.

103 Chafer & Walvoord, 74.

104 LaHaye & Hinson, 166-167.

105 MacDonald, 1810.

106 LaHaye & Hinson, 311.

107 Chafer & Walvoord, 78.

108 LaHaye & Hinson, 118 & 167-168.

109 Webster's Dictionary

110 Walvoord & Zuck, *The Bible Knowledge Commentary: New Testament*, 469.

111 LaHaye & Hinson, 177-178.

112 LaHaye & Hinson, 178.

113 LaHaye & Hinson, 178.

114 LaHaye & Hinson, 178-179.

115 LaHaye & Hinson, 179.

116 Chafer & Walvoord, 316.

117 Walvoord & Zuck, *The Bible Knowledge Commentary: Old Testament*, 1364.

118 Lockyer, 68.

119 Walvoord & Zuck, *The Bible Knowledge Commentary: Old Testament*, 1364-1365.

120 Walvoord & Zuck, 77.

121 Walvoord & Zuck, *The Bible Knowledge Commentary: New Testament*, 77.

122 LaHaye & Hinson, 387.

123 John Phillips, *Exploring Revelation: An Expository Commentary*. (Grand Rapids: Kregel Publications, 2001) 117-118.

124 LaHaye & Hinson, 334.

125 Phillips, *Exploring Revelation*, 121.

126 Phillips, *Exploring Revelation*, 121.

127 MacDonald, 2366.

128 Morris, 18.

129   Webster's Dictionary

130   MacDonald, 2368.

131   Merriam-Webster's Dictionary

132   Phillips, *Exploring Revelation*, 168-169.

133   LaHaye & Hindson, 204.

134   MacDonald, 2371.

135   LaHaye & Hinson, 335-336

136   Morris, 144.

137   Lockyer, 903.

138   MacDonald, 2366.

139   LaHaye & Hindson, 207.

140   LaHaye & Hindson, 207.

141   Wikipedia, org.

142   Chafer & Walvoord, 334.

143   LaHaye & Hinson, 36.

144   LaHaye & Hinson, 234-235.

145   LaHaye & Hinson, 126.

146   Walvoord & Zuck, 147.

147   www.definitions.net

148   Lockyer, 189.

149   LaHaye, 295-297, 299.

150   LaHaye & Hinson, 128.

151   MacDonald, 1545.

152   Phillips, *Exploring Revelation*, 247-248.

153   Phillips, *Exploring Revelation*, 248.

154   Phillips, *Exploring Revelation*, 251.

155   Phillips, *Exploring Revelation*, 248.

156   Dr. David Jeremiah, *The Prophecy Answer Book*, (Nashville: Thomas Nelson, 2010) 177.

157   Jeremiah, 177-189.

158   Walvoord & Zuck, *The Bible Knowledge Commentary: New Testament*, 986.

# BIBLIOGRAPHY

Chafer, Lewis Sperry & Walvoord, John F. *Major Bible Themes.* Grand Rapids: Zondervan Publishing House, 1974.

Galan, Benjamin & Ashby, Brent. *Rose Guide to the Tabernacle.* Torrance: Bristol Works Inc., 2008.

Greene, Evangelist Oliver B. *The New Birth.* Greenville, Oliver B. Greene, 1966.

LaHaye, Tim. *Jesus, Who is He?* Colorado Springs: Multnomah Books, 1996.

LaHaye, Tim. & Hinson, Ed. *The Popular Encyclopedia of Bible Prophecy.* Eugene: Harvest House Publishers, 2004.

Lockyer, Sr., Herbert. *Nelson's Illustrated Bible Dictionary.* Nashville: Thomas Nelson, 1986.

MacDonald, William. *Believer's Bible Commentary.* Nashville: Thomas Nelson, 1995.

Meyers, Joyce. *Help Me I'm Worried.* Tulsa, Oklahoma: Harrison House, 1998.

Morris, Henry M. *The Genesis Record.* Grand Rapids: Baker Book House, 1976.

Pezzotta, Dr. Anthony. *Truth Encounter.* Foreign Mission Board, SBC., 1996.

Pentecost, J. Dwight. *The Words & Works of Jesus Christ*. Grand Rapids: Zondervan Corporation, 1981.

Phillips, John. *Exploring Romans: An Expository Commentary*. Grand Rapids: Kregel Publications, 2002.

Phillips, John. *Exploring Revelation: An Expository Commentary*. Grand Rapids: Kregel Publications, 2001.

Shepherd, J.W. *The Christ of the Gospels*. Grand Rapids: William B. Eerdmans,

Smith, Hannah Whitall. *Perfect Peace*. Chicago: Moody Press, 2000.

Stanley, Charles F. *The Charles F. Stanley Life Principles Bible*. Nashville: Thomas Nelson, Inc., 2005.

Swindoll, Dr. Charles. *Jesus: The Greatest Life of All*. Nashville: Thomas Nelson, 2008.

Thiessen, Henry Clarence. *Lectures in Systematic Theology*. Grand Rapids, William B. Eerdmans Publishing Company, 1979.

USGS, Science for a Changing World; Earthquake Hazards Report.

Walvoord, John F. & Zuck, Roy B. *The Bible Knowledge Commentary*. Colorado Springs: Chariot Victor Publishing, 1983.

http://www.abortionno.org/Resources/fastfacts.html

http://www.blueangels.navy.mil/index.htm

http://www.census.gov/main/www/popclock.html

http://earthquake.usgs.gov/earthquakes/eqinthenews/2010/

http://www.humanillnesses.com/original/A-As/The-Human-Body-Systems-Working-Together.html

http://en.wikipedia.org/wiki/Old_Faithful_Geyser

The Bible Scriptures are taken from the New King James Version Edition (NKJV). Nelson Bibles.

## ABOUT THE AUTHOR

Lisa Underwood Magro, the daughter of a Baptist minister, was raised in a Christian home where, as she says, "Church was not optional." Her parents took her and her two brothers to Sunday services – including Sunday School and Training Union – and Wednesday night services. Lisa is a born again Christian and her love for Jesus is contagious. She has continued going to church throughout her adult life and now teaches women's Bible studies at Bayside Baptist Church in Chattanooga, Tennessee, where she resides with her husband and two stepsons.

"After a couple of years of knowing that the Lord was calling me into ministry, I realized that ministry was to teach women," she says. "Prior to this, I had taught women's water aerobics. I had been teaching women to exercise physically, but God wanted me to teach them spiritually as well."

Lisa says the calling was crystal clear. Her grandmother, who had taught women in Sunday School for 50 years at Center Grove Baptist Church, was in the hospital. It was to be her last hospital stay for she soon went home to be with the Lord. One day while Lisa was visiting her at the hospital, her neighbor called and asked her to speak to her women's group that following Saturday morning at her home. She did. Since then, she has been teaching women at Bayside Baptist Church.

Lisa holds a Doctor of Theology Degree from Covington Theological Seminary.